AF540632

MECHANISM OF FOREST BIOME

MECHANISM OF FOREST BIOME

By

Dr. H. Shivanna

Professor & Head

Deptt. of Forest Biology & Tree Improvement

College of Forestry

SIRSI, Uttar Kannada

(Karnataka)

(India)

DISCOVERY PUBLISHING HOUSE PVT. LTD.

NEW DELHI-110 002

Published by:
Tilak Wasan
DISCOVERY PUBLISHING HOUSE PVT. LTD.
4383/4B, Ansari Road, Darya Ganj
New Delhi-110 002 (India)
Phone : +91-11-23279245, 43596064-65
Fax : +91-11-23253475
E-mail : discoverypublishinghouse@gmail.com
sales@discoverypublishinggroup.com
parul.wasan@gmail.com
web : www.discoverypublishinggroup.com

***First Edition:* 2013**

ISBN: 978-93-5056-280-2

Mechanism of Forest Biome

Printed at:
Dynamic Printers
Delhi

Preface

Forest Biomes represent the largest and most ecologically complex systems. They contain a wide assortment of trees, plants, mammals, reptiles, amphibians, invertebrates, insects and micro-organisms which vary depending on the zone's climates. Sadly, boreal and rainforest biomes are being cut down at an alarming rate, with hundreds of species of plants and animals disappearing from the planet on a daily basis. Forests represent a third of the earth's land, and are found in the four corners of the globe. The major attribute of the forest biome is its trees. While they are different from animals in many ways, they share one common characteristic: they breathe. While humans and animals breathe in oxygen and exhale carbon dioxide, trees take in carbon dioxide and produce oxygen. Deforestation represents a great threat to the future of the earth's atmosphere, and the only way this can be avoided is by careful management of this resource. Once a tree is cut down, another should take its place, but there is still too large a number of trees being cut down as opposed to the number of trees being planted.

Today, forests occupy approximately one-third of Earth's land area, account for over two-thirds of the leaf area of land plants, and contain about 70 per cent of carbon present in living things. They have been held in reverence in folklore and worshipped in ancient religions. However, forests are becoming major casualties of civilization as human populations have increased over the past several thousand years, bringing deforestation, pollution, and industrial usage problems to this important biome.

About 420 million years ago, during the Silurian Period, ancient plants and arthropods began to occupy the land. Over the millions of years that followed, these land colonizers developed and adapted to their new habitat. The first forests were dominated by giant horsetails, club mosses, and ferns that stood up to 40 feet tall.

Life on Earth continued to evolve, and in the late Paleozoic, gymnosperms appeared. By the Triassic Period (245-208 mya), gymnosperms dominated the Earth's forests. In the Cretaceous Period (144-65 mya), the first flowering plants (angiosperms) appeared. They evolved together with insects, birds, and mammals and radiated rapidly, dominating the landscape by the end of the Period. The landscape changed again during the Pleistocene Ice Ages — the surface of the planet that had been dominated by tropical forests for millions of years changed, and temperate forests spread in the Northern Hemisphere.

Present-day forest biomes, biological communities that are dominated by trees and other woody vegetation can be classified according to numerous characteristics, with seasonality being the most widely used.

—Author

Contents

1 Introduction

Today, forests occupy approximately one-third of Earth's land area, account for over two-thirds of the leaf area of land plants, and contain about 70 per cent of carbon present in living things. They have been held in reverence in folklore and worshipped in ancient religions. However, forests are becoming major casualties of civilization as human populations have increased over the past several thousand years, bringing deforestation, pollution, and industrial usage problems to this important biome.

About 420 million years ago, during the Silurian Period, ancient plants and arthropods began to occupy the land. Over the millions of years that followed, these land colonizers developed and adapted to their new habitat. The first forests were dominated by giant horsetails, club mosses, and ferns that stood up to 40 feet tall.

Life on Earth continued to evolve, and in the late Paleozoic, gymnosperms appeared. By the Triassic Period (245-208 mya), gymnosperms dominated the Earth's forests. In the Cretaceous Period (144-65 mya), the first flowering plants (angiosperms) appeared. They evolved together with insects, birds, and mammals and radiated rapidly, dominating the landscape by the end of the Period. The landscape changed again during the Pleistocene Ice Ages — the surface of the planet that had been dominated by tropical forests for millions of years changed, and temperate forests spread in the Northern Hemisphere.

Present-day forest biomes, biological communities that are dominated by trees and other woody vegetation can be classified according to numerous characteristics, with seasonality being the most widely used. Distinct forest types also occur within each of these broad groups.

There are three major types of forests, classed according to latitude:

1. Tropical
2. Temperate
3. Boreal forests (taiga)

Tropical Forest

Tropical forests are characterized by the greatest diversity of species. They occur near the equator, within the area bounded by latitudes 23.5° N and 23.5° S. One of the major characteristics of tropical forests is their distinct seasonality: winter is absent, and only two seasons are present (rainy and dry). The length of daylight is 12 hours and varies little.

- Temperature is on average 20-25° C and varies little throughout the year: the average temperatures of the three warmest and three coldest months do not differ by more than 5°.
- Precipitation is evenly distributed throughout the year, with annual rainfall exceeding 2000 mm.
- Soil is nutrient-poor and acidic. Decomposition is rapid and soils are subject to heavy leaching.
- Canopy in tropical forests is multilayered and continuous, allowing little light penetration.
- *Flora is highly diverse:* one square kilometre may contain as many as 100 different tree species. Trees are 25-35 m tall, with buttressed trunks and shallow roots, mostly evergreen, with large dark green leaves. Plants such as orchids, bromeliads, vines (lianas), ferns, mosses, and palms are present in tropical forests.

- Fauna include numerous birds, bats, small mammals, and insects.

Further subdivisions of this group are determined by seasonal distribution of rainfall:

- *Evergreen rainforest:* no dry season.
- *Seasonal rainforest:* short dry period in a very wet tropical region (the forest exhibits definite seasonal changes as trees undergo developmental changes simultaneously, but the general character of vegetation remains the same as in evergreen rainforests).
- *Semievergreen forest:* longer dry season (the upper tree story consists of deciduous trees, while the lower story is still evergreen).
- *Moist/dry deciduous forest (monsoon):* the length of the dry season increases further as rainfall decreases (all trees are deciduous).

More than one half of tropical forests have already been destroyed.

Temperate Forest

Temperate forests occur in eastern North America, northeastern Asia, and western and central Europe. Well-defined seasons with a distinct winter characterize this forest biome. Moderate climate and a growing season of 140-200 days during 4-6 frost-free months distinguish temperate forests.

- Temperature varies from -30° C to 30° C.
- Precipitation (75-150 cm) is distributed evenly throughout the year.
- Soil is fertile, enriched with decaying litter.
- Canopy is moderately dense and allows light to penetrate, resulting in well-developed and richly diversified understory vegetation and stratification of animals.
- Flora is characterized by 3-4 tree species per square kilometre. Trees are distinguished by broad leaves that are lost annually and include such species as oak,

hickory, beech, hemlock, maple, basswood, cottonwood, elm, willow, and spring-flowering herbs.

- Fauna is represented by squirrels, rabbits, skunks, birds, deer, mountain lion, bobcat, timber wolf, fox, and black bear.

Further subdivisions of this group are determined by seasonal distribution of rainfall:

- *Moist conifer and evergreen broad-leaved forests*: wet winters and dry summers (rainfall is concentrated in the winter months and winters are relatively mild).
- *Dry conifer forests*: dominate higher elevation zones; low precipitation.
- *Mediterranean forests*: precipitation is concentrated in winter, less than 1000 mm per year.
- *Temperate coniferous*: mild winters, high annual precipitation (greater than 2000 mm).
- *Temperate broad-leaved rainforests*: mild, frost-free winters, high precipitation (more than 1500 mm) evenly distributed throughout the year. Only scattered remnants of original temperate forests remain.

Boreal Forest (Taiga)

Boreal forests, or taiga, represent the largest terrestial biome. Occuring between 50 and 60° north latitudes, boreal forests can be found in the broad belt of Eurasia and North America: two-thirds in Siberia with the rest in Scandinavia, Alaska, and Canada. Seasons are divided into short, moist, and moderately warm summers and long, cold, and dry winters. The length of the growing season in boreal forests is 130 days.

- Temperatures are very low.
- Precipitation is primarily in the form of snow, 40-100 cm annually.
- Soil is thin, nutrient-poor, and acidic.
- Canopy permits low light penetration, and as a result, understory is limited.

- Flora consist mostly of cold-tolerant evergreen conifers with needle-like leaves, such as pine, fir, and spruce.
- Fauna include woodpeckers, hawks, moose, bear, weasel, lynx, fox, wolf, deer, hares, chipmunks, shrews, and bats.

Current extensive logging in boreal forests may soon cause their disappearance.

Forest Biomes represent the largest and most ecologically complex systems. They contain a wide assortment of trees, plants, mammals, reptiles, amphibians, invertebrates, insects and micro-organisms which vary depending on the zone's climates. Sadly, boreal and rainforest biomes are being cut down at an alarming rate, with hundreds of species of plants and animals disappearing from the planet on a daily basis. Forests represent a third of the earth's land, and are found in the four corners of the globe. The major attribute of the forest biome is its trees. While they are different from animals in many ways, they share one common characteristic: they breathe. While humans and animals breathe in oxygen and exhale carbon dioxide, trees take in carbon dioxide and produce oxygen. Deforestation represents a great threat to the future of the earth's atmosphere, and the only way this can be avoided is by careful management of this resource. Once a tree is cut down, another should take its place, but there is still too large a number of trees being cut down as opposed to the number of trees being planted.

The largest of the land biomes is the boreal, or Taiga biome. Taiga biomes can be found in areas with shorter, warm summers and long winters; there are Taiga Biomes in Europe, Asia, Siberia, and North-America. Because of the cold climates, plant life in the boreal forest is sturdy, consisting mainly of evergreens and other resilient vegetation. Because the forests' canopy is dense, forest floor vegetation is thin. Animal life in the boreal forest consists mainly of birds and mammals, such as deer, wolves, and various rodents, and very few reptiles. Most of the boreal forests' creatures are well adapted to the cold climate, and hibernate during the long winters.

Temperate Deciduous Forest

Temperate deciduous forest are a close relative of the Taiga biome, and can be found in areas with a milder, shorter winter season. In addition to evergreens, trees in the temperate forest include maple, elm, oak, cedar and other trees which shed their leaves in the fall. The temperate forest's soil in richer than that of the boreal forests' and features a larger assortment of forest floor plan life; this is also due to the fact that the forests' canopy is thinner, allowing more light and heat to penetrate, permitting photosynthesis in the forest floor plants, and the survival of smaller, and cold blooded animals such as garter snakes, turtles, and a few amphibians. Again, several of the temperate forests' species hibernate, and/or burrow in the ground to pass the winter months.

Other forests which fall between the boreal and temperate classification include moist evergreen forests, moist evergreen and broad-leaf forests, dry evergreen forests, mediterranean forests, temperate evergreen forests, and temperate broad-leaf forests.

Forests can be found in all regions capable of sustaining tree growth, at altitudes up to the tree line, except where natural fire frequency or other disturbance is too high, or where the environment has been altered by human activity.

The latitudes 10° north and south of the Equator are mostly covered in tropical rainforest, and the latitudes between 53° N and 67° N have boreal forest. As a general rule, forests dominated by angiosperms (*broadleaf forests*) are more species-rich than those dominated by gymnosperms (*conifer*, *montane*, or *needleleaf forests*), although exceptions exist.

Forests sometimes contain many tree species only within a small area (as in tropical rain and temperate deciduous forests), or relatively few species over large areas (e.g., taiga and arid montane coniferous forests). Forests are often home to many animal and plant species, and biomass per unit area is high compared to other vegetation communities. Much of this biomass occurs below ground in the root systems and as partially decomposed plant detritus. The woody component of a forest contains lignin, which is relatively slow to decompose compared with other organic materials such as cellulose or carbohydrate.

Forests are differentiated from woodlands by the extent of canopy coverage: in a forest, the branches and the foliage of separate trees often meet or interlock, although there can be gaps of varying sizes within an area referred to as forest. A woodland has a more continuously open canopy, with trees spaced farther apart, which allows more sunlight to penetrate to the ground between them.

Temperate Needleleaf

Temperate needleleaf forests mostly occupy the higher latitude regions of the northern hemisphere, as well as high altitude zones and some warm temperate areas, especially on nutrient-poor or otherwise unfavourable soils. These forests are composed entirely, or nearly so, of coniferous species (Coniferophyta). In the Northern Hemisphere pines Pinus, spruces Picea, larches Larix, silver firs Abies, Douglas firs Pseudotsuga and hemlocks Tsuga, make up the canopy, but other taxa are also important. In the Southern Hemisphere, most coniferous trees (members of the Araucariaceae and Podocarpaceae) occur in mixtures with broadleaf species that are classed as broadleaf and mixed forests.

Temperate broadleaf and mixed forests include a substantial component of trees in the Anthophyta. They are generally characteristic of the warmer temperate latitudes, but extend to cool temperate ones, particularly in the southern hemisphere. They include such forest types as the mixed deciduous forests of the United States and their counterparts in China and Japan, the broadleaf evergreen rainforests of Japan, Chile and Tasmania, the sclerophyllous forests of Australia, central Chile, the Mediterranean and California, and the southern beech Nothofagus forests of Chile and New Zealand.

Tropical Moist Forests

Tropical moist forests include many different forest types. The best known and most extensive are the lowland evergreen broadleaf rainforests include, for example: the seasonally inundated várzea and igapó forests and the terra firma forests of the Amazon Basin; the peat swamp forests and moist dipterocarp forests of Southeast Asia; and the high forests of the Congo Basin. The forests of tropical mountains are also included in this broad category, generally divided into upper and lower montane formations on the basis of their physiognomy, which varies with altitude. The montane forests include cloud forest, those forests at middle to high altitude, which derive a significant part of their water budget from cloud, and support a rich abundance of vascular and nonvascular epiphytes. Mangrove forests also fall within this broad category, as do most of the tropical coniferous forests of Central America.

Tropical Dry Forests

Tropical dry forests are characteristic of areas in the tropics affected by seasonal drought. The seasonality of rainfall is usually reflected in the deciduousness of the forest canopy, with most trees being leafless for several months of the year. However, under some conditions, e.g. less fertile soils or less predictable drought regimes, the proportion of evergreen species increases and the forests are characterised as "sclerophyllous". Thorn forest, a dense forest of low stature with a high frequency of thorny or spiny species, is found where drought is prolonged, and especially where grazing animals are plentiful. On very poor soils, and especially where fire is a recurrent phenomenon, woody savannas develop.

Sparse Trees and Parkland Forests

Sparse trees and parkland are forests with open canopies of 10-30 per cent crown cover. They occur principally in areas of transition from forested to non-forested landscapes. The two major zones in which these ecosystems occur are in the boreal region and in the seasonally dry tropics. At high latitudes, north of the main zone of boreal forest or taiga, growing conditions are not adequate to maintain a continuous closed forest cover, so tree cover is both sparse and discontinuous. This vegetation is variously called open taiga, open lichen woodland, and forest tundra. It is species-poor, has high bryophyte cover, and is frequently affected by fire.

Forest Plantations

Forest plantations, generally intended for the production of timber and pulpwood increase the total area of forest worldwide. Commonly mono-specific and/or composed of introduced tree species, these ecosystems are not generally important as habitat for native biodiversity. However, they can be managed in ways that enhance their biodiversity protection functions and they are important providers of ecosystem services such as maintaining nutrient capital, protecting watersheds and soil structure as well as storing carbon. They may also play an important role in alleviating pressure on natural forests for timber and fuelwood production.

Temperate and Boreal Forest Types

- *Evergreen needleleaf forest:* Natural forest with > 30 per cent canopy cover, in which the canopy is predominantly (> 75%) needleleaf and evergreen.
- *Deciduous needleleaf forests:* Natural forests with > 30 per cent canopy cover, in which the canopy is predominantly (> 75%) needleleaf and deciduous.
- *Mixed broadleaf/needleleaf forest:* Natural forest with > 30 per cent canopy cover, in which the canopy is composed of a more or less even mixture of needleleaf and broadleaf crowns (between 50:50% and 25:75%).
- *Broadleaf evergreen forest:* Natural forests with > 30 per cent canopy cover, the canopy being > 75 per cent evergreen and broadleaf.

- *Deciduous broadleaf forest:* Natural forests with > 30 per cent canopy cover, in which > 75 per cent of the canopy is deciduous and broadleaves predominate (> 75% of canopy cover).
- *Freshwater swamp forest:* Natural forests with > 30 per cent canopy cover, composed of trees with any mixture of leaf type and seasonality, but in which the predominant environmental characteristic is a waterlogged soil.
- *Sclerophyllous dry forest:* Natural forest with > 30 per cent canopy cover, in which the canopy is mainly composed of sclerophyllous broadleaves and is > 75 per cent evergreen.
- *Disturbed natural forest:* Any forest type above that has in its interior significant areas of disturbance by people, including clearing, felling for wood extraction, anthropogenic fires, road construction, etc.
- *Sparse trees and parkland:* Natural forests in which the tree canopy cover is between 10-30 per cent, such as in the steppe regions of the world. Trees of any type (e.g., needleleaf, broadleaf, palms).
- *Exotic species plantation:* Intensively managed forests with > 30 per cent canopy cover, which have been planted by people with species not naturally occurring in that country.
- *Native species plantation:* Intensively managed forests with > 30 per cent canopy cover, which have been planted by people with species that occur naturally in that country.

* *Unspecified forest plantation:* Forest plantations showing extent only with no further information about their type, This data currently only refers to the Ukraine.

* *Unclassified forest data:* Forest data showing forest extent only with no further information about their type.

Those * marked have been created as a result of data holdings which do not specify the forest type, hence some categories are quoted here:

- *Lowland evergreen broadleaf rain forest:* Natural forests with > 30 per cent canopy cover, below 1,200 m (3,937 ft) altitude that display little or no seasonality, the canopy being >75 per cent evergreen broadleaf.
- *Lower montane forest:* Natural forests with > 30 per cent canopy cover, between 1200-1800 m altitude, with any seasonality regime and leaf type mixture.
- *Upper montane forest:* Natural forests with > 30 per cent canopy cover, above 1,800 m (5,906 ft) altitude, with any seasonality regime and leaf type mixture.
- *Freshwater swamp forest:* Natural forests with > 30 per cent canopy cover, below 1,200 m (3,937 ft) altitude, composed of trees with any mixture of leaf type and seasonality, but in which the predominant environmental characteristic is a waterlogged soil.
- *Semi-evergreen moist broadleaf forest:* Natural forests with > 30 per cent canopy cover, below 1,200 m (3,937 ft) altitude in which between 50-75 per cent of the canopy is evergreen, > 75 per cent are broadleaves, and the trees display seasonality of flowering and fruiting.
- *Mixed broadleaf/needleleaf forest:* Natural forests with > 30 per cent canopy cover, below 1,200 m (3,937 ft) altitude, in which the canopy is composed of a more or less even mixture of needleleaf and broadleaf crowns (between 50:50% and 25:75%).
- *Needleleaf forest:* Natural forest with > 30 per cent canopy cover, below 1,200 m (3,937 ft) altitude, in which the canopy is predominantly (> 75%) needleleaf.
- *Mangroves:* Natural forests with > 30 per cent canopy cover, composed of species of mangrove tree, generally along coasts in or near brackish or seawater.
- *Disturbed natural forest:* Any forest type above that has in its interior significant areas of disturbance by people, including clearing, felling for wood extraction, anthropogenic fires, road construction, etc.
- *Deciduous/semi-deciduous broadleaf forest:* Natural forests with > 30 per cent canopy cover, below 1,200 m

(3,937 ft) altitude in which between 50-100 per cent of the canopy is deciduous and broadleaves predominate (> 75% of canopy cover).

- *Sclerophyllous dry forest:* Natural forests with > 30 per cent canopy cover, below 1,200 m (3,937 ft) altitude, in which the canopy is mainly composed of sclerophyllous broadleaves and is > 75 per cent evergreen.
- *Thorn forest:* Natural forests with > 30 per cent canopy cover, below 1,200 m (3,937 ft) altitude, in which the canopy is mainly composed of deciduous trees with thorns and succulent phanerophytes with thorns may be frequent.
- *Sparse trees and parkland:* Natural forests in which the tree canopy cover is between 10-30 per cent, such as in the savannah regions of the world. Trees of any type (e.g., needleleaf, broadleaf, palms).
- *Exotic species plantation:* Intensively managed forests with > 30 per cent canopy cover, which have been planted by people with species not naturally occurring in that country.
- *Native species plantation:* Intensively managed forests with > 30 per cent canopy cover, which have been planted by people with species that occur naturally in that country.

The scientific study of forest species and their interaction with the environment is referred to as forest ecology, while the management of forests is often referred to as forestry. Forest management has changed considerably over the last few centuries, with rapid changes from the 1980s onwards culminating in a practice now referred to as sustainable forest management. Forest ecologists concentrate on forest patterns and processes, usually with the aim of elucidating cause and effect relationships. Foresters who practice sustainable forest management focus on the integration of ecological, social and economic values, often in consultation with local communities and other stakeholders.

Anthropogenic factors that can affect forests include logging, urban sprawl, human-caused forest fires, acid rain, invasive species, and the slash and burn practices of swidden agriculture or shifting cultivation. The loss and re-growth of forest leads to a distinction between two broad types of forest, primary or old-growth forest and secondary forest. There are also many natural factors that can cause changes in forests over time including forest fires, insects, diseases, weather, competition between species, etc. In 1997, the World Resources Institute recorded that only 20 per cent of the world's original forests remained in large intact tracts of undisturbed forest. More than 75 per cent of these intact forests lie in three countries - the Boreal forests of Russia and Canada and the rainforest of Brazil. In 2006 this information on intact forests was updated using latest available satellite imagery.

Canada has about 4,020,000 square kilometres (1,550,000 sq mi) of forest land. More than 90 per cent of forest land is publicly owned and about 50 per cent of the total forest area is allocated for harvesting. These allocated areas are managed using the principles of sustainable forest management, which includes extensive consultation with local stakeholders. About eight per cent of Canada's forest is legally protected from resource development (Global Forest Watch Canada) (Natural Resources Canada). Much more forest land — about 40 per cent of the total forest land base — is subject to varying degrees of protection through processes such as integrated land use planning or defined management areas such as certified forests (Natural Resources Canada).

By December 2006, over 1,237,000 square kilometres of forest land in Canada (about half the global total) had been certified as being sustainably managed (Canadian Sustainable Forestry Certification Coalition). Clearcutting, first used in the latter half of the 20th century, is less expensive, but devastating to the environment and companies are required by law to ensure that harvested areas are adequately regenerated. Most Canadian provinces have regulations limiting the size of clearcuts, although some older clearcuts can range upwards of 110 square kilometres (27,000 acres) in size which were cut over several years. China instituted a ban on logging, beginning in 1998, due to the destruction caused by clearcutting. Selective cutting avoids the erosion, and flooding, that result from clearcutting.

In the United States, most forests have historically been affected by humans to some degree, though in recent years improved forestry practices has helped regulate or moderate large scale or severe impacts. However, the United States Forest Service estimates a net loss of about two million hectares (4,942,000 acres) between 1997 and 2020; this estimate includes conversion of forest land to other uses, including urban and suburban development, as well as afforestation and natural reversion of abandoned crop and pasture land to forest. However, in many areas of the United States, the area of forest is stable or increasing, particularly in many northern states. The opposite problem from flooding has plagued national forests, with loggers complaining that a lack of thinning and proper forest management has resulted in large forest fires.

Old-growth forest contains mainly natural patterns of biodiversity in established seral patterns, and they contain mainly species native to the region and habitat. The natural formations and processes have not been affected by humans with a frequency or intensity to change the natural structure and components of the habitat. Secondary forest contains significant elements of species which were originally from other regions or habitats.

The Tropical Rain Forest Biome

The tropical rain forest is a forest of tall trees in a region of year-round warmth. An average of 50 to 260 inches (125 to 660 cm.) of rain falls yearly.

Rain forests belong to the tropical wet climate group. The temperature in a rain forest rarely gets higher than 93°F (34°C) or drops below 68°F (20°C); average humidity is between 77 and 88 per cent; rainfall is often more than 100 inches a year. There is usually a brief season of less rain. In monsoonal areas, there is a real dry season. Almost all rain forests lie near the equator.

Rainforests now cover less than 6 per cent of Earth's land surface. Scientists estimate that more than half of all the world's plant and animal species live in tropical rain forests. Tropical rainforests produce 40 per cent of Earth's oxygen.

A tropical rain forest has more kinds of trees than any other area in the world. Scientists have counted about 100 to 300 species in one 2½-acre (1-hectare) area in South America. Seventy per cent of the plants in the rainforest are trees.

About ¼ of all the medicines we use come from rainforest plants. Curare comes from a tropical vine, and is used as an anesthetic and to relax muscles during surgery. Quinine, from the cinchona tree, is used to treat malaria. A person with lymphocytic leukemia has a 99 per cent chance that the disease will go into remission because of the rosy periwinkle. More than 1,400 varieties of tropical plants are thought to be potential cures for cancer.

All tropical rain forests resemble one another in some ways. Many of the trees have straight trunks that don't branch out for 100 feet or more. There is no sense in growing branches below the canopy where there is little light. The majority of the trees have smooth, thin bark because there is no need to protect the them from water loss and freezing temperatures. It also makes it difficult for epiphytes and plant parasites to get a hold on the trunks. The bark of different species is so similar that it is difficult to identify a tree by its bark. Many trees can only be identified by their flowers.

Despite these differences, each of the three largest rainforests—the American, the African, and the Asian—has a different group of animal and plant species. Each rain forest has many species of monkeys, all of which differ from the species of the other two rain forests. In addition, different areas of the same rain forest may have different species. Many kinds of trees that grow in the mountains of the Amazon rain forest do not grow in the lowlands of that same forest.

Layers of the Rainforest

There are four very distinct layers of trees in a tropical rain forest. These layers have been identified as the emergent, upper canopy, understory, and forest floor.

1. **Emergent** trees are spaced wide apart, and are 100 to 240 feet tall with umbrella-shaped canopies that grow above the forest. Because emergent trees are exposed to drying winds, they tend to have small, pointed leaves. Some species lose their leaves during the brief dry season in monsoon rainforests. These giant trees have straight, smooth trunks with few branches. Their root system is very shallow, and to support their size they grow buttresses that can spread out to a distance of 30 feet.

2. The upper canopy of 60 to 130 foot trees allows light to be easily available at the top of this layer, but greatly reduced any light below it. Most of the rainforest's animals live in the upper canopy. There is so much food available at this level that some animals never go down to the forest floor. The leaves have 'drip spouts' that allows rain to run off. This keeps them dry and prevents mold and mildew from forming in the humid environment.
3. The understory, or lower canopy, consists of 60 foot trees. This layer is made up of the trunks of canopy trees, shrubs, plants and small trees. There is little air movement. As a result the humidity is constantly high. This level is in constant shade.
4. The forest floor is usually completely shaded, except where a canopy tree has fallen and created an opening. Most areas of the forest floor receive so little light that few bushes or herbs can grow there. As a result, a person can easily walk through most parts of a tropical rain forest. Less than one per cent of the light that strikes the top of the forest penetrates to the forest floor. The top soil is very thin and of poor quality. A lot of litter falls to the ground where it is quickly broken down by decomposers like termites, earthworms and fungi. The heat and humidity further help to break down the litter. This organic matter is then just as quickly absorbed by the trees' shallow roots.

Plant Life

Besides these four layers, a shrub/sapling layer receives about three per cent of the light that filters in through the canopies. These stunted trees are capable of a sudden growth surge when a gap in the canopy opens above them.

The air beneath the lower canopy is almost always humid. The trees themselves give off water through the pores (stomata) of their leaves. This process, called transpiration, can account for as much as half of the precipitation in the rain forest.

Rainforest plants have made many adaptations to their environment. With over 80 inches of rain per year, plants have made adaptations that helps them shed water off their leaves quickly so the branches don't get weighed down and break. Many plants have drip tips and grooved leaves, and some leaves have oily coatings to shed water. To absorb as much sunlight as possible on the dark understory, leaves are very large. Some trees have leaf stalks that turn with the movement of the sun so they always absorb the maximum amount of light. Leaves in the upper canopy are dark green, small and leathery to reduce water loss in the strong sunlight. Some trees will grow large leaves at the lower canopy level and small leaves in the upper canopy. Other plants grow in the upper canopy on larger trees to get sunlight. These are the epiphytes such as orchids and bromeliads. Many trees have buttress and stilt roots for extra support in the shallow, wet soil of the rainforests.

Over 2,500 species of vines grow in the rainforest. Lianas start off as small shrubs that grow on the forest floor. To reach the sunlight in the upper canopy it sends out tendrils to grab sapling trees. The liana and the tree grow towards the canopy together. The vines grow from one tree to another and make up 40 per cent of the canopy leaves. The rattan vine has spikes on the underside of its leaves that point backwards to grab onto sapling trees. Other 'strangler' vines will use trees as support and grow thicker and thicker as they reach the canopy, strangling its host tree. They look like trees whose centers have been hollowed out.

Dominant species do not exist in tropical rainforests. Lowland dipterocarp forest can consist of many different species of Dipterocarpaceae, but not all of the same species. Trees of the same species are very seldom found growing close together. This bio diversity and separation of the species prevents mass contamination and die-off from disease or insect infestation. Bio diversity also insures that there will be enough pollinators to take care of each species' needs.

Animals depend on the staggered blooming and fruiting of rainforest plants to supply them with a year-round source of food.

Animal Life

Many species of animal life can be found in the rain forest. Common characteristics found among mammals and birds (and reptiles and amphibians, too) include adaptations to a life in the trees, such as the prehensile tails of New World monkeys. Other characteristics are bright colours and sharp patterns, loud vocalizations, and diets heavy on fruits.

Insects make up the largest single group of animals that live in tropical forests. They include brightly coloured butterflies, mosquitoes, camouflaged stick insects, and huge colonies of ants.

The Amazon River Basin Rainforest

The Amazon river basin rainforest contains a wider variety of plant and animal life than any other biome in the world. The second largest population of plant and animal life can be found in scattered locations and islands of Southeast Asia. The lowest variety can be found in Africa. There may be 40 to 100 different species in 2.5 acres (1 hectare) of a tropical rain forest.

When early explorers first discovered the rainforests of Africa, Southeast Asia and South America, they They were amazed by the dense growth, trees with giant buttresses, vines and epiphytes. The tropical vegetation grew so dense that it was difficult to cut one's way through it. It was thought at the time that the soil of a rainforest must be very fertile, filled with nutrients, enabling it to support the immense trees and other vegetation they found.

Today we know that the soil of the tropical rainforests is shallow, very poor in nutrients and almost without soluble minerals. Thousands of years of heavy rains have washed away the nutrients in the soil obtained from weathered rocks. The rainforest has a very short nutrient cycle. Nutrients generally stay in an ecosystem by being recycled and in a rainforest are mainly found in the living plants and the layers of decomposing leaf litter. Various species of decomposers like insects, bacteria, and fungi make quick work of turning dead plant and animal matter into nutrients. Plants take up these nutrients the moment they are released.

A study in the Amazon rainforest found that 99 per cent of nutrients are held in root mats. When a rainforest is burned or cut down the nutrients are removed from the ecosystem. The soil can only be used for a very short time before it becomes completely depleted of all nutrients.

The tropical rain forest can be found in three major geographical areas around the world.

1. Central America in the the Amazon river basin.
2. Africa - Zaire basin, with a small area in West Africa; also eastern Madagascar.
3. Indo-Malaysia - west coast of India, Assam, Southeast Asia, New Guinea and Queensland, Australia.

In an average year the climate in a tropical rain forest is very humid because of all the rainfall. A tropical rainforest gets about 150 cm of rain per year. It gets lots of rain because it is very hot and wet in rain forests. The hotter the air, the more water vapor it can hold. It rains usually about 1/8 of an inch per day.

This climate is found near the equator. That means that there is more direct sunlight hitting the land and sea there than anywhere else. The sun warms the land and sea and the water evaporates into the air. The warm air can hold a lot of water vapor. As the air rises, it cools. That means it can hold less water vapour. Then as warm meets cold, condensation takes place and the vapor forms droplets and clouds form. The clouds then produce rain. It rains more than ninety days a year and the strong sun usually shines between the storms. The water cycle repeats often along the equator.

The main plants in this biome are trees. This is important because in the rain forest, some rain never gets past the trees and to the smaller plants and ground below. Trees in this climate reach a height of more than 164 feet. They form a canopy. The forest floor is called understory. The canopy also keeps sunlight from reaching the plants in the understory. Between the canopy and understory is a lower canopy made up of smaller trees. These plants do receive some filtered sunlight.

The tropical rain forest is classified under the Köppen Classification system as *Af*, meaning tropical forest. The *A* is given to tropical climates that are moist for all months and which have average temperatures above 18° Celsius. The *f* stands for sufficient precipitation for all months. The latitude range for my climate is 15° to 25° North and South of the equator.

The annual precipitation of a rain forest is greater than 150 cm. In a rain forest there is a short dry season. In only a month the rainforest receives 4 inches of rain. The rain forest climate is different from a lot of other climates. In other climates, the evaporation is carried away to fall as rain in far off areas, but in the rain forests, 50 per cent of the precipitation comes from its own evaporation. A lot of the rain that falls on the rain forest never reaches the ground, instead it stays on the trees because the leaves act as a shield.

The average temperature of a rain forest is about 77° Fahrenheit. The rain forest is about the same temperature year round. The temperature never drops below 64° Fahrenheit. Rain forests are so hot because they are found near the equator. The closer to the equator you are, the more solar radiation there is. The more solar radiation there is, the hotter it is. Rain forest are never found in climates which have temperatures 32° and below because the plant life will not be able to live in the frost. All the plants will die out if the rain forest is cooler.

The plants that make up the understory of a rain forest have adapted to the small amount of sunlight that they receive. Ferns and mosses do well, along with epiphytes. These are plants that grow on other plants. They can be found growing on branches of tall trees. There are many different plant species found in the rain forest.

3 Coniferous Forest Biome

'Coniferous' is a word that means 'coming from the cones'. Coniferous forests consist chiefly of trees that produce cones: Pines, Spruces, and Cedars primarily. The 'cones' the trees produce contain seeds which the cones' weight prevents from traveling far from the parent tree. The cones are designed to roll about three linear feet when they fall to the ground and then become wedged into the soil. This is nature's way of insuring that the conifers (cone-producing trees) grow in orderly rows, instead of crowding each other out competing for sunlight. In this way, the trees grow nicely to about ceiling height while keeping the pleasing triangular shape that makes them sought-after holiday trees.

Coniferous forests can be found worldwide, mostly between 86 and 98 north latitude. There are some seventeen billion square miles of coniferous forests in the world.

Though it's true that the coniferous forests of the world support some animal species— like weasels, the lynx and foxes— the biome is important mainly as the habitat for prized Christmas Trees. Imagine what your December would be like without a fragrant tree culled from one of the worlds' coniferous forests. Conifer oils are also important, being used to produce pine-based cleaning products and pine-scented car air fresheners. Realizing this, environmentalists and scientists have been vigilant in protecting habitat for our

our pines, spruces and cedars; especially the Blue Spruce and Scotch Pine which both look great with tinsel and hold up well, even when laden with heavier ornaments.

MAJOR PLANT AND ANIMAL LIFE SUPPORTED BY CONIFEROUS FORESTS

Plant Life

- Scotch Pine
- Blue Spruce
- Norway Pine
- Mistletoe
- Red Cedar
- Blue Cedar
- Holly Bush
- Prickers
- Scrub Pine

Animal

- Grey Wolf
- Yellow-jacket
- Pine-Tar Vole
- Field Mouse
- Jack rabbit
- Lynx
- Wood-Duck
- Reindeer Weasel

Moist Temperate Coniferous Forest Biome

The moist temperate coniferous forest of the Pacific Northwest includes the area from the coastal ranges of northern California (below 5000 ft. elevation) to the southern coast of Alaska (below 2000 ft.). Because of its proximity to the Pacific Ocean, the climate is mild and without temperature extremes. Precipitation varies from 50 inches per year in the southern portion of the biome, where relatively dry summers prevail, to 200 inches on the mountain slopes of Washington and southern British Columbia.

The fogbelt, comprising the southern part of the biome from San Francisco to southern Oregon, is dominated by redwoods (*Sequoia sempervirens*). Stands are situated on moist river flats and in sheltered valleys, where evapotranspirational losses are minimized. New and higher roots are produced in reaction to continued deposition of alluvial material at the bases of the tall trunks, which often surpass 250 feet in height. The thick bark, which affords protection against insects, pathogens, and fire, is thought to contribute to the great longevity (1,000-2,000 years) of individuals.

To the north of the redwoods in Oregon and southern Washington, where the soil is well drained and precipitation is slightly lower, grow extensive, pure stands of the subclimax species.

Douglas-fir (*Pseudotsuga menziesii*). On the Olympic Peninsula, where it reaches its maximum development (often approach ing 10 feet in diametre and 300 feet in height), Douglas-fir is found in association with Sitka spruce (*Picea sitchensis*), western redcedar (*Thuja plicata*), and western hemlock (*Tsuga heterophylla*). In the south it mixes with sugar pine (*Pinus lambertiana*), incense cedar (*Libocedrus docurrens*), and ponderosa pine (*Pinus ponderosa*).

The sandy and gravelly soils along rivers and streams of this biome are frequently lined with narrow groves of red alder (*Alnus rubra*), black cottonwood (*Populus trichocarpa*), and bigleaf maple (*Acer macrophyllum*). Both bigleaf maple and red alder (a nitrogen fixer) are also pioneer tree species on recently burned and heavily logged areas in the region.

Northward in the Puget Sound area (and in particular the Olympic Peninsula), a climax forest of western hemlock, western redcedar, and Pacific silver fir (*Abies amabilis*) dominates the landscape. Sitka spruce, Alaska-cedar (*Chamaecyparis nootkatensis*), and mountain hemlock (*Tsuga mertensiana*) are common associates. At higher altitudes, these species are joined by grand fir (*A. grandis*), and on drier sites by Douglas-fir. The dense canopy of these forests precludes the growth of all but a few species in the herb and shrub layers where cover is sparse. Due to the prevailing moisture-laden winds, there is a partial extension of this forest association into the western slopes of the Rocky Mountains in Idaho and British Columbia. Western larch (*Larix occidentalis*) and western white pine (*Pinus monticola*) are important successional species in this eastern extension.

The Mountain Complex Biome

The mountain complex biome refers to the totality of vegetation types and associated animals which occupy the mountains and high plateaus of western North America.

Elevational transects extending over several thousand feet may exhibit vegetation ranging from desert to alpine tundra. The type of plant community which will dominate a given altitude is dependent on three interrelated factors of the physical environment: *(i)* steepness and orientation of slope with respect to incoming solar radiation; *(ii)* composition of the soil; and amount of available moisture.

On a more regional basis, precipitation and temperature vary considerably, depending on latitude and the location and orientation of mountain masses relative to the prevailing westerlies and relative to other mountain masses. Thus, we see that timberline decreases in altitude with increasing latitude in both the Rockies and Pacific Coast mountains, but that at a given latitude timberline is lower in the coastal mountains than in the Rockies. The effects of orographic precipitation are seen in the dramatic shifts in vegetation from the windward to leeward sides of mountain masses.

Southern Rockies (Arizona)

The *mountain complex of the southern Rockies* is exemplified in the vegetation of the San Francisco Mountains of northern Arizona, which reach altitudes in excess of 12,000 feet. The zonation of flora ranges from desert species at the lowest elevations (where rainfall is low and evapotranspiration rates are high), through Douglas-fir and spruce-fir forests at the middle elevations (where moisture from orographic precipitation is high), to alpine vegetation at the highest points (where low temperatures becomes a limiting factor).

The *creosote bush-greasewood association* (*Larcea divaricata* and *Sarcobatus vermiculatus*, respectively) occupies the hot, dry lower slopes below 6000 feet. Once desert grassland, this area was severely overgrazed by sheep and cattle.

The range between 5000 and 7000 feet is occupied by the *pinyon-juniper association*. The area is characterized by an environment of alkaline soils, low rainfall and humidity, high wind movement, intense sunlight and high evapotranspiration rates. The stands of slow growing, sparsely spaced trees range from pure pinyon (*Pinus cembroides*) to pure juniper (*Juniperus* spp.), probably depending upon available seed source as much as on geographical location and local environmental conditions.

The *Douglas-fir zone* is situated in the 7500-9000 feet elevational range. The area of overlap of the ponderosa pine and Douglas-fir zones is commonly referred to as the lower montane forest. Compared to lower zones, daily temperature fluctuations in the Douglas-fir zone are smaller, the average temperature is somewhat lower, and humidity is significantly higher. The Rocky Mountain variety of Douglas-fir (*Pseudotsuga menziesii* var. *glauca*) encountered here is much smaller (and more tolerant in the understory) than its relative in the Pacific Northwest (*P. m.* var. *menziesii*) and usually occurs in mixed stands rather than in pure stands. Common associates include white fir (*Abies concolour*) and blue spruce (*Picea pungens*) on moist sites, and ponderosa pine and lodgepole pine (*Pinus contorta*) on drier sites. The dry exposed ridges of this zone are commonly occupied by limber pine (*Pinus flexilis*) and bristlecone pine (*P. aristata*).

In the cold, humid environment above the Douglas-fir zone, between 8,500 and 11,500 feet, is the *spruce-fir zone*, dominated by Engelmann spruce (*Picea engelmannii*) and subalpine fir (*Abies lasiocarpa*). In the lower and middle parts of the range, subalpine fir occupies sites too wet, too dry or too low in nutrients for Engelmann spruce to grow. At higher elevations it is not uncommon to find pure stands of Engelmann spruce. As in the lower montane forest, limber and bristlecone pines occupy the dry, exposed, south-facing ridges and slopes. Many of the bristlecone pines are over 4000 years old.

Krummholz

Krummholz is the name given to the dwarfed and stunted trees that occupy the transition zone between the spruce-fire zone and alpine tundra. The environment is characterized by intense solar radiation, high winds and large diurnal temperature fluctuations.

The *alpine tundra* zone occurs above timberline where climate is even more severe than that in the Krummholz. Short grasses (*Poa* spp., *Festuca* spp.), sedges (*Carex* spp.), tiny alpine flowers, and rocky outcrops dominate the landscape.

Above the tundra lie the mountain tops, a land of perpetual ice and snow. The complete lack of soil and the severe environmental conditions combine to make colonization by even the hardiest invaders an impossibility.

Alpine meadows occur in depressions sheltered by hills or open areas surrounded by trees. Large amounts of snow accumulate and with the mositure provided by the 'spring' melt (late June-early July) showy wildflowers come to dominate the landscape.

Lodgepole pine, a prolific seeder with serotinous cones, and quaking aspen, a prolific seeder and sprouter, are particularly well-adapted to fire, and are among the first to successfully invade a burn, almost regardless of altitude or latitude. Aspen is also common in areas of major soil disturbances, such as ravines swept by avalanches. Narrow leaf cottonwood (*Populus angustifolia*) is commonly found along the stream banks of this region and the lower plains.

Northern Rockies

In the northern U.S., timberline decreases in altitude, as do the various accompanying vegetational zones. There is also a major change in species in some of the higher zones due to a wind corridor through the Cascades. This corridor allows moisture bearing winds from the Pacific to reach the western slopes of the Rockies, resulting in a wetter, milder climate than would normally be expected. Because of this, mountain hemlock (*Tsuga mertensiana*) is found growing with Engelmann spruce and subalpine fir (*Abies lasiocarpa*) in the higher altitudes. Western hemlock, western redcedar, and grand fir are found in the Douglas-fir zone. Western larch and western white pine (*Pinus monticola*) are the two principal successional species of the latter zone, both germinating and growing well on mineral seedbeds prepared by fire and other major disturbances.

Whitebark pine (*Pinus albicaulis*) is characteristic of the dry ridges and exposed areas of high altitudes. Its flexible branches allow it to withstand heavy snow loads but often the snow, coupled with extreme wind and cold, force the whitebark into its familiar, prostrate, ground-hugging form. The cones of the whitebark, unlike the other pines, fall from the trees and disintegrate, forming a fertile oasis among the thin, bare soils of the mountain top in which its seeds can germinate.

In the Canadian Rockies the *subalpine zone* is by far the most extensive, covering nearly all of the mountains. In the northern part of this range, white spruce of the northern forest is commonly found in association with subalpine fir.

Sierra Nevadas

Physically, the Sierra Nevada Mountains range from northern to southern California, but floristically vegetation extends into the Cascade range of southern Oregon. The Sierras are oriented in a north-south direction, perpendicular to the prevailing westerly winds, and thus show distinct patterns of orographic precipitation. The west slopes of the Sierras rise gradually from the Great Valley, receiving very little precipitation; heavy rains fall near mid-slope as a result of condensation of cool moist air. The abrupt drop to the Great Basin on the east slope is very dry as the moisture-depleted air provides little precipitation.

The foothills of the west slopes form an *open woodland* between 500-2500 feet. Blue oak (*Quercus douglasii*) is the dominant tree, but is often found in association with digger pine (*Pinus sabiniana*).

The *montane forest* ranges from 2000-6000 feet in the southern Cascades and from 5000-8000 feet in the southern Sierras. There are six primary species in this zone, occurring either in pure stands or in various combinations. White fir is the dominant species at the higher altitudes in the zone where winters are long and snows are heavy; it is seldom found in pure stands.

Pure stands of incense cedar (*Libocedrus decurrens*) dominate the richest sites in the lower sections of the zone. Ponderosa pine tends to dominate the lower margins of the zone since it is the most drought resistant of the six species. Jeffrey pine (*Pinus jeffreyi*), a close relative of ponderosa pine, has a higher tolerance for cold and frost and thus is commonly found in depressions and flats where cold air tends to gather, and at the upper extremes of the ponderosa pine zone where temperatures are much colder. Sugar pine reaches its maximum development in the middle of the montane zone where the climate is less extreme.

Douglas-fir (*Pseudotsuga menziesii* var. *menziesii*) tends to dominate the more moist, northern regions. A less common but more famous associate of these central montane species is the giant sequoia (*Sequoia gigantea*). The species occurs in scattered clumps throughout central California where annual precipitation is relatively high (40-60 inches) and soils are well drained. Until recently, the primary danger of these 'sentinels of the Sierras' (many of 30 feet in diametre and 250 feet in height) was soil compaction resulting from tourism. The limited aeration destroyed the fibrous root system of the tree and altered water-holding properties of the soil, resulting in decreased vigor. Chaparral species commonly invade drier sites in the zone following fires.

The *subalpine zone* extends approximately 2000 feet above the upper montane limit. The climate consists of long winters with heavy snows and short, dry summers with cool temperatures. Red fir (*Abies magnifica*) is the major climax species here, often occurring in pure, even-aged stands. At the upper end of the subalpine zone red fir mixes with Jeffrey, western white and lodgepole pines. The latter is an important fire-related successional species. White fir and mountain hemlock are less common associates.

Near the timber line, whitebark, limber and foxtail pines are the dominant species, often occurring in scattered clumps interspersed by alpine meadows. These are all small tree species, rarely surpassing 30 feet in height, limited by the severe environment and poor soil conditions.

The *subalpine zone of the east slope* is comprised mainly of timber line species of the western slope—whitebark, limber and foxtail pines. Lodgepole pine grows quite extensively on these eastern slopes, as it does throughout most of the West. Red fir occurs only in scattered areas.

Jeffrey pine is the dominant species in the *montane zone of the east slopes*. Here it forms open park-like stands, similar to, but in place of, the ponderosa pine of the western Sierras.

Cascade Mountains

The Cascades extend from southern Oregon to British Columbia. The western slopes are generally considered to be part of the moist temperate coniferous forest biome, with which they were included and discussed in this treatment of biomes. However, above 5000 feet there exists a subalpine forest of mountain hemlock, noble fir (*Abies procera*), subalpine fir, and pacific silver fir (*A. anabilis*). Timber line here occurs near 6000 feet, much lower than at the same latitude in the Rockies. This is attributed primarily to the heavier snow loads experienced in the Cascades.

The *eastern slopes of the Cascades* are drier than the west and have species similar to those of the northern Rockies. The subalpine forest is much the same as on the western slopes. The upper montane forest consists of Douglas-fir, western hemlock, and western redcedar. Western larch and western white pine are the common successional species following fire.

The *lower slopes of the eastern Cascades* are especially dry, with rainfall ranging from 10-40 inches per year, and a long dry summer dominating the climate. In this area, ponderosa pine thrives in vast, pure stands. This tree has a long, fast-growing tap root that allows it to reach a more constant water supply than that available to most plants.

Regeneration of ponderosa pine is also particularly successful because the seedlings are able to withstand prolonged drought by obtaining moisture from the night dew.

Interior British Columbia

In the interior of British Columbia, the Pacific Coast mountains and the Rockies merge. Here the land takes the shape of a high, rolling plateau that is covered by a forest of white spruce, Douglas-fir, lodgepole pine and aspen. Farther to the north these species are replaced by an association of lodgepole pine, subalpine fir, and Englemann spruce. In northern British Columbia, the Yukon, and Alaska the forest changes to white spruce and subalpine fir. White spruce is the primary successional species on the nutrient rich sites, while black spruce (*Picea mariana*) forms an edaphic climax on the bogs.

Coniferous Swamp

Coniferous swamps are forested wetlands in which the dominant trees are lowland conifers such as northern white cedar (*Thuja occidentalis*). The soil in these swamp areas are typically saturated for most of the growing season and are occasionally inundated by seasonal storms or winter snow melt.

The substrate is usually organic in nature and may contain peat in varying amounts or be composed entirely of muck. The swamp substrate is typically nutrient rich and neutral to alkaline but can be acidic and nutrient poor.

Coniferous swamps vary in composition, with different species of conifer dominating, and varying amounts of deciduous hardwoods growing within the swamp. A wide diversity of plants are represented within the swamp with certain species dominating in a variety of microhabitats dependent on factors such as available sunlight as in cases of trees downed by wind or disease, soil Ph, standing groundwater and differences of elevation within the swamp such as tussocks and nurse logs.

The different types of coniferous swamps are referred to according to their dominant trees *rich conifer swamp* dominated by Northern white-cedar which typically occur south of the climatic tension zone throughout the Midwest and northeastern United States and adjacent areas in Canada. North of the climatic tension zone, tamarack (*Larix laricina*) is the dominant species of conifer in minerotrophic wetlands, classified as a *rich tamarack swamp*. A roughly equal mix of hardwood trees and conifers a known as a *hardwood-conifer swamp.*

Variety of Both Evergreen and Deciduous Trees

A variety of both evergreen and deciduous trees may be present in the rich conifer swamp in addition to the dominant species.

Trees

- *Thuja occidentalis* Northern white cedar, the dominant conifer, also known as arborvitae a common landscape specimen in northern U.S. states and Canada.
- *Abies balsamea* Balsam fir
- *Acer rubrum* Red maple
- *Betula papyrifera Paper birch)*
- *Cornus stolonifera Red-osier dogwood*
- *Cornus florida Flowering dogwood*
- *Larix laricina* Tamarack
- *Picea mariana* Black spruce
- *Picea glauca* White spruce
- *Pinus strobus* White pine
- *Tsuga canadensis* Hemlock
- *Ulmus americana* American elm
- *Populus tremuloides Quaking aspen*
- *Populus balsamifera* Balsam poplar

Shrubs

- *Alnus rugosa* Tag elder
- *Ilex verticillata* Winterberry
- *Ilex mucronata* Mountain holly
- *Sambucus racemosa* Red elderberry

- *Gaylussacia baccata Huckleberry*
- *Taxus canadensis* Canadian yew
- *Lonicera canadensis American fly honeysuckle*
- *Lonicera oblongifolia Swamp fly honeysuckle*
- *Vaccinium angustifolium* Low sweet blueberry
- *Vaccinium myrtilloides* Canada blueberry
- *Ribes americanum* Wild black currant
- *Ribes triste* Swamp red currant
- *Ribes lacustre* Swamp black currant

Vines

- *Toxicodendron radicans* Poison ivy
- *Lonicera dioica* Limber honeysuckle

Ferns

- *Osmunda cinnamomea* Cinnamin fern
- *Thelypteris palustris* Marsh fern
- *Osmunda spectabilis* Royal fern
- *Gymnocarpium dryopteris* Oak fern

Gramminoids

A variety of grasses and sedges may be present including multiple varieties of *carex.*

- *Glyceria striata* (Fowl manna grass)

Mosses

- *Callicladium haldanianum* Callicladium moss
- *Sphagnum centrale*

Orchids

- *Cypripedium calceolus* Yellow lady's-slipper
- *Platanthera hyperborea* Tall northern bog orchid

Forbs

- *Aquilegia canadensis* (Red Columbine)

Freshwater Swamp Forests

Freshwater swamp forests, or flooded forests, are forests which are inundated with freshwater, either permanently or seasonally. They normally occur along the lower reaches of rivers and around freshwater lakes. Freshwater swamp forests are found in a range of climate zones, from boreal through temperate and subtropical to tropical.

In the Amazon Basin of Brazil, a seasonally flooded forest is known as a *várzea*, a use that now is becoming more widespread for this type of forest in the Amazon (though generally spelled *varzea* when used in English). *Igapó*, another word used in Brazil for flooded Amazonian forests, is also sometimes used in English. Specifically, varzea refers to whitewater-inundated forest, and igapo to blackwater-inundated forest.

Peat swamp forests are swamp forests where waterlogged soils prevent woody debris from fully decomposing, which over time creates a thick layer of acidic peat.

FRESHWATER SWAMP FOREST ECOREGIONS

Afrotropic

- Eastern Congolian swamp forests (Democratic Republic of the Congo)
- Niger Delta swamp forests (Nigeria)
- Western Congolian swamp forests (Republic of the Congo, Democratic Republic of the Congo)

Australasia

- Northern New Guinea lowland rain and freshwater swamp forests (Indonesia, Papua New Guinea)
- Southern New Guinea freshwater swamp forests (Indonesia, Papua New Guinea)

Indomalaya

- Borneo peat swamp forests (Brunei, Indonesia, Malaysia)
- Chao Phraya freshwater swamp forests (Thailand)
- Irrawaddy freshwater swamp forests (Myanmar)
- Peninsular Malaysian peat swamp forests (Malaysia, Thailand)
- Red River freshwater swamp forests (Vietnam)
- Southwest Borneo freshwater swamp forests (Indonesia)
- Sundarbans freshwater swamp forests (Bangladesh)

- Tonle Sap-Mekong peat swamp forests (Cambodia, Vietnam)

Neotropic

- Cantão igapó forest (Brazil)
- Gurupa varzea (Brazil)
- Iquitos varzea (Bolivia, Brazil, Peru)
- Marajó varzea (Brazil)
- Monte Alegre varzea (Brazil)
- Orinoco Delta swamp forests (Guyana, Venezuela)
- Pantanos de Centla (Mexico)
- Paramaribo swamp forests (Guyana, Suriname)
- Purus varzea (Brazil)

Bangladesh

Ratargul Fresh Water Swamp Forest

The Temperate Deciduous Forest Biome

The temperate deciduous forest biome occupies most of the eastern part of the United States and a small strip of southern Ontario. Precipitation varies from 28 inches per year in the northwestern section of the biome to 60 inches per year in the southeastern part; in most areas the precipitation is distributed evenly throughout the year. Frost occurs throughout the biome, and summer and winter are distinct seasons.

The dominant plant species of the biome are broad-leaved deciduous trees. Because the biome covers such a large geographical area, large differences have led to the recognition of eight major forest regions within the biome, each dominated by a different species or association of species. These are: mixed mesophytic, Appalachian oak, hemlock-white pine-northern hardwoods, oak-hickory, maple-basswood, beech-maple, oak-pine, and southern pine.

Mixed Mesophytic Forest Region

The mixed mesophytic forest region is in the centrally located and topographically diverse Appalachian and Cumberland Plateaus. Geologically, it is the oldest region in the biome and is the most complex and highly developed biotically. Nearly all the dominant species in the entire biome are found here, and many reach their maximum development here. The mixed mesophytic region is thought to be the center of dispersal from which the other forest regions in the biome were formed. In all, there are about 30 tree species which assume dominance in the region; however, in most areas dominance is shared by two or three of these species, depending on differences in microclimate and other factors. Yellow buckeye (*Aesculus octandra*) and white basswood (*Tilia heterophylla*) are the most constant dominants and are considered the indicator species for the region. Other common dominants include yellow-poplar (*Liriodendron tulipifera*), American beech (*Fagus grandifolia*), cucumber magnolia (*Magnolia acuminata*), sugar maple (*Acer saccharum*), white oak (*Quercus alba*), and eastern hemlock (*Tsuga canadensis*).

Appalachian Oak Forest

The Appalachian oak forest region lies to the east, north, and southeast of the mixed mesophytic forest. Geologically, it is characterized by a system of parallel valleys and ridges. Northern red oak (*Quercus rubra*) and white oak are the two major species in the region.

White oak reaches its maximum development on deep, rich soils of coves and high bottomlands, but grows well on all but the driest and wettest sites in the region. The success of white oak is attributed to its ability to survive for long periods as an understory species, its quick and vigorous response to release from this suppression, and its great longevity (often reaching 400-600 years). The ecologically similar red oak occupies sites which are usually slightly drier or wetter than those dominated by white oak. Chestnut oak (*Q. prinus*) is a third important species of the region and forms an edaphic climax with post oak (*Q. stellata*) and blackjack oak (*Q. marilandica*) on rocky, dry ridges. The American chestnut (*Castanea dentata*) was another important dominant in the region until eliminated by a bark fungus in the early 1900's. Sugar maple is the climax species on very rich sites, while American beech dominates the cove forests too moist for white oak and tulip-poplar. Pitch pine (*Pinus rigida*) is a common successional species.

Hemlock-white Pine-northern Hardwood Region

The hemlock-white pine-northern hardwood region is situated along the northern edge of the biome, bordering the northern coniferous forest. Eastern hemlock (*Tsuga canadensis*) is one of the most tolerant of all trees and survives under very low light conditions. Eastern white pine is varied in its occurrence with other species and in its ecological role in the region. In the Lake States it often forms extensive pure stands of on drier sites mixes with red pine and jack pine. On heavier soils characteristic of the East, it occurs mainly as scattered individuals amongst a predominantly hardwood forest. Sugar maple, American beech, white ash (*Fraxinus americana*) and yellow birch (*Betula alleghaniensis*) are the most common hardwoods in the region. Paper birch (*B. papyrifera*) is a common early successional species in the eastern part of the region, while aspen (*Populus tremuloides* and *P. grandidentata*) and jack pine assume this role in the Lake States (along with paper birch).

Oak-hickory Forest Region

The oak-hickory forest region occupies drier areas to the west of the mixed mesophytic forest region. Drought-resistant oaks and hickories are the most common trees species. The principal oaks are white oak, northern red oak, and black oak (*Q. velutina*), while bur oak (*Q. macrocarpa*), blackjack oak, shingle oak (*Q. imbricaria*) and overcup oak (*Q. lyrata*) are also common. The most important hickories are bitternut (*Carya cordiformis*) and shagbark (*C. ovata*), while shellbark (*C. laciniosa*), mockernut (*C. tomentosa*), and pignut (*C. glabra*) occur more frequently on the drier upland soils. The trees commonly found scattered throughout the stream and river valleys of the region (and indeed nearly all regions in the biome) are American elm (*Ulmus americana*), American sycamore (*Platanus occidentalis*), hackberry (*Celtis* spp.), silver maple (*Acer saccharinum*), river birch (*Betula nigra*), and eastern cottonwood (*Populus deltoides*). These riparian trees are generally fast-growing, shallow-rooted, relatively large, and able to withstand repeated floodings throughout the year. A savanna-like transition zone is formed along the western edge of the oak-hickory region where the temperate deciduous forest biome grades into the temperate grasslands biome. Here bur oak, the most drought resistant of all (eastern) oaks, occurs as scattered trees amongst the grassy plains.

Maple-basswood Forest

The maple-basswood forest region, encompassing lower Minnesota, northeastern Iowa, and western Wisconsin, comprises the northwestern corner of the temperate deciduous forest. Sugar maple and American basswood (*Tilia americana*) are the major tree species within this region. Sugar maple is a prolific seeder, while basswood is a vigorous sprouter—properties which coupled with their understory tolerance, help account for the dominance of these species. Other important tree species in the region include boxelder (*Acer negundo*), blue ash (*Fraxinus quadrangulata*), and northern red oak. Bur oak and bitternut hickory occupy sites lower in nutrients.

Beech-maple Forest Region

The beech-maple forest region is found almost entirely within Indiana and northern Ohio.

American beech, similar to the codominant sugar maple in shade tolerance and most environmental requirements, prefers slightly moister sites. Because of its thin bark and shallow root system, beech is especially susceptible to fire injury, sunscald, and winter cracking. Other important species in the beech-maple region include black cherry (*Prunus serotina*), yellow birch, American ash, black walnut (*Juglans nigra*), tullip-poplar, red elm (*Ulmus rubra*), northern red oak, and, in the southern section, Ohio buckeye (*Aesculus glabra*). Shagbark hickory and various oaks occupy dry sites throughout the region.

Oak-pine Region

The *oak-pine region* occupies an area between the hardwoods of the Appalachians and the pure pines of the southlands. Generally speaking, half of this forest is comprised of hardwoods, primarily upland oaks, while the other half is a mixture of loblolly, shortleaf and Virginia pines (*P. taeda, P. echinata*, and *P. virginiana*, respectively). The dominant hardwoods are white oak, post oak, shagbark hickory, mockernut hickory, pignut hickory, and sweetgum.

Southern Pine Region

The southern pine region occupies an area comprised of the Gulf and Atlantic Coastal Plains, plus the Piedmont of the eastern and southern Appalachians. In spite of the dominance of pines, the natural climax vegetation is considered to be hardwoods. Throughout much of the southern U.S., the lands now occupied by pines were abandoned after a period of intensive use (farming, surface mining, etc.) and allowed to revert back to natural conditions. Most of these lands are highly eroded, with little of the A1 soil horizon remaining. A typical successional sequence on such lands in the Piedmont might be:

1. Annual and perennial weedy forbs and grasses (crabgrass, goldenrod, asters, horseweed, ragweed and buttonweed)
2. Broomsedge (a perennial grass)
3. Woody invaders (eastern redcedar (*Juniperus virginiana*), sassafras (*Sassafras albidum*), winged elm [(*Ulmus alata*), persimmon (*Diospyros virginiana*)]
4. Southern pines (primarily loblolly and shortleaf)
5. Oaks and hickories.

This process of secondary succession may take several hundred years.

North-east Asian Deciduous Forests

Several 'subregions' of the southern pine region can be defined on the basis of the dominant species. The Virginia pine subregion occupies the northern Piedmont and Appalachian foothills. Virginia pine, the most drought-resistant of the southern pines, is a pioneer species on impoverished soils. It is often found in association with pitch pine (*P. rigida*). The *shortleaf-loblolly pine subregion* occupies the Piedmont south of the oak-pine region. The climate is humid, with long hot summers and mild winters; soils are predominantly sandy.

Pure stands of loblolly pine are commonly found where drainage is poor; by contrast, shortleaf pine is found on soils which are better drained and of lower nutrient content. The *longleaf-slash pine subregion* is found along the Gulf Coastal Plains and into central Florida. Over 50 per cent of the forest stands in the subregion are comprised of these two species, generally with slash pine on the wet sites and long leaf pine on the drier sites.

Fire plays an important role in maintaining this seral pine stage, primarily by reducing hardwood competition and by controlling plant diseases. This is particularly evident in longleaf pine, which may be held in the grass stage for prolonged periods in the absence of fire.

The *s*crubland subregion is situated on white sands near the coast where soils are acidic, highly leached, very low in nutrients, and extremely droughty. On undisturbed sites a scrub oak community, composed primarily of live, turkey, and blackjack oaks (*Quercus virginia, Q. laevis*, and *Q. marilandica*, respectively) forms the natural vegetation. Spanish bayonet (*Yucca* spp.), a monocot, is also common here.

In areas undisturbed by fire, lie thick forests of saw-palmetto (*Serenoa repens*), the most abundant of the native palms and a monocot. Pine stands of sand pine (*Pinus clausa*) are often found on sites extremely low in nutrients. This species closely resembles jack pine of the Lake States, with one of its varieties having serotinous cones typical of 'fire species'. Southern magnolia (*Magnolia grandiflora*) is likely to be found on moist, well-drained sites in association with nearly all the southern oaks, tulip-poplar, sweetgum, the ashes, and the hickories.

Appalachian Mountains

The Appalachian Mountains, trending roughly north-south, traverse the eastern part of the biome. The relatively high altitudes allow northern species to penetrate far more deeply into the South than would normally be possible. There is also somewhat of an altitudinal zonation of plant associations in the southern Appalachians, with oak-hickory-pine occupying lower elevations and dry sites; mixed mesophytic forests occurring in moist, sheltered coves; northern hardwoods dominating the 3500-4500 ft. elevational range; and northern coniferous forests occupying the highest areas.

Deciduous forests can be found in the eastern half of North America, and the middle of Europe. There are many deciduous forests in Asia. Some of the major areas that they are in are southwest Russia, Japan, and eastern China. South America has two big areas of deciduous forests in southern Chile and Middle East coast of Paraguay. There are deciduous forests located in New Zealand, and southeastern Australia also.

The average annual temperature in a deciduous forest is 50° F. The average rainfall is 30 to 60 inches a year.

In deciduous forests there are five different zones. The first zone is the Tree Stratum zone. The Tree Stratum zone contains such trees as oak, beech, maple, chestnut hickory, elm, basswood, linden, walnut, and sweet gum trees. This zone has height ranges between 60 feet and 100 feet.

The small tree and sapling zone is the second zone. This zone has young, and short trees. The third zone is called the shrub zone. Some of the shrubs in this zone are rhododendrons, azaleas, mountain laurel, and huckleberries. The Herb zone is the fourth zone. It contains short plants such as herbal plants. The final zone is the Ground zone. It contains lichen, club mosses, and true mosses.

The deciduous forest has four distinct seasons, spring, summer, autumn, and winter. In the autumn the leaves change colour. During the winter months the trees lose their leaves.

The animals adapt to the climate by hibernating in the winter and living off the land in the other three seasons. The animals have adapted to the land by trying the plants in the forest to see if they are good to eat for a good supply of food. Also the trees provide shelter for them. Animal use the trees for food and a water sources. Most of the animals are camouflaged to look like the ground.

The plants have adapted to the forests by leaning toward the sun. Soaking up the nutrients in the ground is also a way of adaptation.

A lot of deciduous forests have lost land to farms and towns. Although people are trying to protect the forests some poachers are trying to kill the animals in the forests. The animals are losing their homes because of people building their homes.

The word 'Deciduous' means 'falling off or out at a certain season'. That explains why deciduous forest means a forest in which the leaves fall off the trees when the winter comes.

The deciduous forests are located in the temperate zone above the tropical forests and below the coniferous forests. Most of Europe, the eastern half of North America, parts of Japan and Asia were once covered with large deciduous forests. Most of the deciduous forests have now disappeared but many of the trees still grow in deciduous forest biome. The types of trees you can find in these three regions are broad leafed deciduous trees and some of the evergreen species. The trees are more commonly known as ash, oak, lime, beech, birch and northern arrowwood. Also found in this biome are wild flowers such as oxlip, bluebells, painted trillium and primrose. As well as things such as carpet moss, tawny milk-cap mushrooms and lady fern.

The soil is very fertile. In fact, some of the great agricultural regions are found in this biome. That is one of the reasons there aren't a lot of original deciduous forests left in the world. Almost all of the forests in North America are second growth forests but it still has the biggest variety of original plant species. In Europe there are only a few species of original trees left. Most of the forests have been cleared for agriculture. China has been clearing the natural trees for at least 4,000 years and most of the forests are man-made.

There are many types of animals in the deciduous forest ranging from mammals like deer to bugs like mosquitoes. Many of the animals are either nut and acorn feeders, or omnivores. Many of the animals have adapted to forest life. Some of them hibernate during the winter months.

A few common animals found in the deciduous forest are, deer, gray squirrels, mice raccoons, salamanders, snakes, robins, frogs and many types of insects. Some animals migrate south when winter comes.

Most deciduous forests are found in Eastern North America somewhere around 35-48° N, and Europe and Asia around 45-60° N. There are some deciduous regions in the southern hemisphere but their plants and animals are different from those of the northern deciduous forests.

The average temperature is around 50° F (about 10° C). The average rainfall is 30-60 inches (75-150 cm) per year. You can find all four seasons: winter (cold and frosty), summer (hot and humid), fall (cool and breezy), and spring (warm and breezy). There is about a 6 month growing season.

Boreal Forest or Taiga Biome

Climate in the Taiga

Climate in the taiga is cold, with average annual temperatures from about +5 to –5 C. I always find it interesting to note that one location with a coniferous forest, Yellowstone National Park in Wyoming, has an average annual temperature of only 1 C Precipitation varies, from about 20 cm of precipitation per year to over 200 cm. Much of the precipitation, of course, is in the form of snow. The winters are cold and long; summers are relatively short and cool. With snowmelt and low temperatures, there is little evaporation in the summer, so the ground is usually very moist during the growing season. Add to the availability of water the fact that the short summer has extremely long day length at the northerly latitudes and you have a situation for explosive plant growth in the summer. Still the growing season is short, usually less than three months.

The boreal forests, which extend in broad bands across North America and Eurasia. The boreal forest, also known as Taiga, a Russian word that recognizes the swampy nature of much of this forest in the summer, lies to the south of the tundra and to the north of deciduous forests and grasslands. There is no comparable zone in the southern hemisphere, probably because there is little land area there with the proper climate (cold temperatures in the southern hemisphere being moderated by close proximity to the sea; at high latitudes in the southern hemisphere most land is relatively close to the ocean, unlike the northern hemisphere.

Also, circulation of the oceans in the southern hemisphere is not blocked by the continental land masses to the same extent as it is in the north. It should be noted that a similar coniferous forests exist on some mountains of the alpine biome; on this map the southern extension of the boreal forests into eastern North America along the Appalachian Mountains is shown, while the coniferous forests of the western North American mountains is not.

Many plant species are found in the Taiga, but coniferous trees are obviously the dominant plant form. These trees shed snow easily, and they retain their needles through the winter. The needles themselves are well-adapted, with thick waxy coatings and small surface area, to resist cold conditions and minimize water loss, an important consideration even in the swampy taiga where water may be frozen much of the year. Together, these adaptations mean that even in cool conditions, if the temperature rises above freezing during the day photosynthesis can proceed. Broadleaf plants usually lose their leaves at the onset of freezing conditions in the fall and will not regrow them until most of the danger of frost has passed. This means that the growing season of broad-leafed trees is much shorter than it is for coniferous trees, and the advantage the coniferous trees gain allows them to dominate in the cold taiga climate (note that broad leaves are much more efficient, so if conditions are favorable (warm and moist) they are the preferred leaf type).

Important conifer types include firs and pines (right, with the fir on the left of the image and the pine on the right), spruces, hemlocks, and larches. All of these tree types bear cones of one sort or another (above). The seeds are retained in these structures until they open and cast the seeds out, often from a considerable height. Some species of birds and mammals may also open the cones foraging for the seeds. With two seeds per scale, it is likely that as the animal breaks one seed loose the other will fall free to the forest floor. Some cones do not open until there has been a fire, but since fire is not an important aspect of the taiga that is probably not the case for most taiga conifers.

In addition to the conifers, mosses (above and below) and lichens are also important in the taiga and may be an important part of the diet for many animals. Please note that the species shown here are not necessarily found in the Taiga.

Giant Sequoia (*Sequoiadendron giganteum*) are not really a boreal species (they live in the Sierra Nevada of California, and are probably more of a temperate rainforest species. I put them here because they are neat.

Animal Species in Coniferous Forests

Numerous animal species are found in coniferous forests.

Among the main carnivores of the boreal forest are a number of felids (cats) and canids (dogs). The cats range in size from the Siberian Tiger, down through the lynx to the bobcat. The Amur (Siberian) Tigers are but one subspecies of this large Asian cat which is known from the tropics of India and Indonesia all the way north to the boreal forests of Russia.

The Bobcat is a much smaller cat with a range that extends far into the temperate zone, unlike its larger and more northerly relative the lynx.

Herbivores range in size from the large members of the deer family such as the Elk to insects on the small end of the scale. The name Elk needs some explanation. In Europe, the term Elk is applied to what we in North America would call a moose, and the animal they call a Red Deer is probably in the same species as our Elk. To avoid at least some confusion, a number of authorities in the United States and Canada have begun using a Native American name, Wapiti, in place of the name Elk (of course, scientists use the scientific name *Cervus elaphus* and avoid ALL confusion).

Among the smaller mammalian herbivores are the arboreal (tree-living) Porcupine and the terrestrial Snowshoe Hare. The Snowshoe Hare pictured here is just beginning its winter transformation; the brown coat that camouflaged it so well in the summer and fall is beginning to be shed and replaced with white fur that will help hide it in the winter snows.

The big story in the taiga is adaptation to winter cold and snow. As seen above, the Snowshoe Hare with its large paws (for running over the snow) and white fur is well adapted for life in the snow. Other animals may burrow beneath the snow and forage for their food in tunnels on and in the forest floor; they are insulated from the worst cold of winter by the snow. Still others will hibernate throughout the winter. The cold, however, does take its toll; compared to temperate forests there are fewer species of plants and animals, and among the animals the cold-blooded amphibians and reptiles are noticeably reduced. Bird species mostly deal with the cold by migrating south during the cold winter and returning in the spring. During the brief summer, the very long days that exist at high latitudes means a lot of photosynthesis can take place, and this profusion of plant growth is accompanied by a burst of insect activity. Birds migrating to the taiga in summer are able to take advantage of the new growth and insect abundance - not to mention the reduced competition in the vast forests - and raise their young.

We've already dealt with how the plants deal with the cold in the section on indicator plants, above. One other aspect of the boreal forest with regard to plants should be mentioned, however. The cold, as well as the acid conditions produced by the fallen conifer needles, reduces the rate of decomposition on the forest floor. This in turn reduces the availability of nutrients in the soils, and competition for nutrients by plants growing in the boreal forest may be stiff. In addition, many of the soils are wet and bog-like during the brief summer when the snow finally melts. In many places, the conditions for plants are more reminiscent of a bog. Carnivory, parasitism, use of mycorrhizae - all of these are just a few of the tricks that are used by boreal forest plants.

Threat to the Boreal Forest

Perhaps the biggest threat to the boreal forest today is exploration and development of oil and natural gas reserves. From Alaska to Canada to Russia, it is estimated that vast amounts of petroleum products lie under these forests. Increased instability in the Middle East, more effective technology for working in the cold, and the high demand for fossil fuels are pushing exploration and development into areas once thought impossible to exploit. It is not clear whether the slow-growing coniferous forests can recover.

Other threats abound. Perhaps the most serious is Global Warming; as the planet warms the southern reaches of the boreal forest will become warm enough for deciduous trees to outcompete the conifers and replace them. It is not clear whether the tundra areas to the north will support forests even under warmer conditions, and it is less clear if the trees will be able to move north rapidly enough in any event. There is some evidence to suggest that additional carbon dioxide and methane - both greenhouse gasses - will be liberated from warmer tundra and taiga soils as the built up detritus of thousands of years is finally free to decompose. This additional release of greenhouse gasses could accelerate global warming even further.

Logging is always a threat; unless carefully managed these forests are very slow to regrow and corporate pressures may reduce the amount of management and/or accelerate cutting beyond what can be sustained. Large areas of boreal forest have also been flooded as part of hydroelectric projects.

National Parks for Tour

Many of the great American National Parks in the west are covered with a coniferous forest that resembles in many ways the boreal forests of the north (above). Yosemite National Park, for instance, mostly lies at an elevation that is cool enough to select for coniferous trees over deciduous ones. These alpine coniferous forests differ from the boreal coniferous forests of the north, however, in a number of important ways. Usually the slopes are steeper and the ground rockier; while the trees may resemble a boreal forest the undergrowth does not.

Mammalian Predators in the Coniferous Forest

Mammalian predators in the coniferous forest range from the small, like the bobcat (above right), which feeds on rodents, hares and other small prey, to the Grizzly (right) which is capable of taking down very large prey indeed (although a surprising majority of their diet consists of plant material, often dug from the ground with the help of the mass of muscles that makes up the characteristic hump of the grizzly's back).

Much of the meet that grizzlies eat may be scavenged from the carcasses of large herbivores killed by winter conditions or other predators, such as wolves. Reading the journals of Lewis and Clark, the first Europeans to encounter the grizzly, one gets the sense that the members of the Corps of Discovery were being stalked as prey by the grizzlies they encountered. It often took several of the best marksmen in the country, armed with the finest weapons of the time, to stop a single bear. It makes one wonder how Native Americans were able to coexist with these bears.

Canids (dogs) are important carnivores in the boreal forest. In North America, the range in size from large (wolves, an expedition is planned for fall 2006 to get pictures of them) to medium (coyotes, see the grassland biome) to small (foxes, pictured here above and left). All of the canids are very adaptable and can be found (or could be found) over a wide range of biomes in North America. Foxes, which prey primarily on small herbivores such as rodents, are well at home in the boreal forests. The Red Fox (above) is found in Europe, North America, Asia (and has been introduced into Australia) and its range extends from the tundra to the tropics, but the boreal forest seems to be an anchor in its range. The Gray Fox, on the other hand, is restricted to North America and is more southern in its distribution, only reaching the fringe of the boreal forest (though it may be more common in alpine coniferous forests).

The Porcupine, below, is well-protected against canid and other predators. Its hindquarters are covered with long barbed quills which penetrate the skin of a predator (particularly near the mouth) and which are difficult to remove once they have attached. The hind view of this porcupine is no accident; with the quills on their backs porcupines quickly turn tail and don't worry too much about close pursuit. They spend much of their time in the trees and feed exclusively on vegetation. Primarily a creature of the north woods, they can also be found in alpine areas, grasslands and even deserts. They do have a few predators, including bobcats and larger members of the weasel family including fishers and wolverines.

The tiny saw-whet owl is sometimes seen in the north woods. In the winter, it may migrate south into temperate forests, but its bread-and-butter hunting grounds are the coniferous forests, including alpine forests in the west. They prefer a forest with at least a few deciduous trees, for these are more likely to harbor boring insects than are the resin-laden conifers. And burrowing insects mean woodpeckers, and woodpeckers mean cavities for the saw-whet owl to nest in. Like most owls, they feed on small mammals such as mice and voles; they may also take small birds, reptiles and amphibians.

The boreal forest and its alpine cousins are host to a wide variety of deer, ranging from the large moose (inset, right) to the whitetail deer. All of these large herbivores prefer the cool forest lest they overheat in the sun, but all need open land on which to graze. Of the deer, moose are perhaps best adapted to wetlands and thrive in the boggy boreal forest. The wapiti prefers mature forest (and more open land in the winter), while thc deer move between forest and grassland constantly. In addition to grass and other ground plants, deer of all types can graze on a variety of plant materials including leaves and berries picked from trees overhead; often these are taken by the deer standing on its hind legs. A forest with too many deer may have a 'browse line' where the height of the deer is demonstrated graphically by the absence of green vegetation anywhere in reach of the deer. Such heavy grazing pressure can dramatically alter plant communities. The moose is also a heavy grazer, but compared to the other species it also spends a lot of its time consuming aquatic plants. Mule Deer and White-tailed deer coexist in the western US (the Mule Deer is not found in the east) with the Mule deer preferring open, dry areas to the moister, more covered areas sought out by the smaller white-tails.

Water plays an important role in the boreal forest (or the alpine forests of the west, for that matter). The Brule River, above, drains a relatively flat boreal forest and the dark brown water carries the stains from the tannins and other plant products produced in the leaves of the species occupying the boggy forest floor.

In contrast, the water drains more quickly from the inclined meadows at Tuolumne in Yosemite (above left), where the water runs more clear. Both streams are relatively free of silt and other evidence of soil erosion; both no doubt swell in the spring with snowmelt runoff.

Birches are among the most cold-tolerant of the deciduous trees and their presence is usually a sign that one is at the boundary of a coniferous and a deciduous forest. Aspens play a similar role in the mountains of the western United States.

Reindeer (Caribou in the New World) are the most northern deer species and are relatively large (but not as big as moose or elk). They frequent not only the tundra (where they are featured here) but the boreal forests as well. it lives far south in Florida it has a much smaller body size. There is a general tendency towards larger body size within a species (or within closely related species) as one moves towards the poles. This apparently has to do with thermo-regulation, larger animals are more efficient at retaining body heat in cold climates, while smaller animals can more easily cool off in warmer climates. The rule is known as Bergman's Rule.

6

Temperate Broadleaf and Mixed Forest

Mixed forests are a temperate and humid biome. The typical structure of these forests includes four layers. The uppermost layer is the canopy composed of tall mature trees ranging from 33 to 66 m (100 to 200 feet) high. Below the canopy is the three-layered, shade-tolerant understory that is roughly 9 to 15 m (30 to 50 feet) shorter than the canopy. The top layer of the understory is the sub-canopy which is composed of smaller mature trees, saplings, and suppressed juvenile canopy layer trees awaiting an opening in the canopy. Below the sub-canopy is the shrub layer, composed of low growing woody plants. Typically the lowest growing (and most diverse) layer is the ground cover or herbaceous layer.

Trees

Characteristic dominant broadleaf trees in this biome include oaks (*Quercus* spp.), beeches (*Fagus* spp.), maples (*Acer* sap.), and birches (*Betula* spp.). The term 'mixed forest' comes from the inclusion of coniferous trees as a canopy component of these forests. Typical coniferous trees include: Pines (*Pinus* spp.), firs (*Abies* spp.), and spruces (*Picea* spp.). In some areas of this biome the conifers may be a more important canopy species than the broadleaf species.

Climate

Temperate broadleaf and mixed forests occur in areas with distinct warm and cool season, which give it a moderate annual average temperature (3 to 15.6 °C). These forests occur in relatively warm and rainy climates, sometimes also with a distinct dry season. A dry season occurs in the winter in East Asia and in summer on the wet fringe of the Mediterranean climate zones. Other areas have a fairly even distribution of rainfall; annual rainfall is typically over 600 millimetres (24 inches) and often over 1500 millimetres (60 inches). Temperatures are typically moderate except in parts of Asia such as Ussuriland where temperate forests can occur despite very harsh conditions with very cold winters.

MIXED FOREST ECOREGIONS

Oceania	
Oceania Temperate Broadleaf and Mixed Forests	
Chatham Islands temperate forests	New Zealand
Eastern Australian temperate forests	Australia
Fiordland temperate forests	New Zealand
Nelson Coast temperate forests	New Zealand
Northland temperate forests	New Zealand
Northland temperate kauri forests	New Zealand
Stewart Island/Rakiura temperate forests	New Zealand
Richmond temperate forests	New Zealand
Southeast Australia temperate forests	Australia
Southland temperate forests	New Zealand
Tasmanian Central Highland forests	Australia
Tasmanian temperate forests	Australia
Tasmanian temperate rain forests	Australia
Westland temperate forests	New Zealand
Eurasia	
Palearctic Temperate Broadleaf and Mixed Forests	
Appenine deciduous montane forests	Italy
Atlantic mixed forests	Belgium Denmark France Germany Netherlands

Azores temperate mixed forests	Portugal
Balkan mixed forests	Bulgaria Greece Macedonia Romania Serbia Turkey
Baltic mixed forests	Denmark Germany Poland Sweden
Cantabrian mixed forests	Portugal Spain
Caspian Hyrcanian mixed forests	Azerbaijan Iran
Caucasus mixed forests	Armenia Azerbaijan Georgia Russia Turkey
Celtic broadleaf forests	Ireland United Kingdom
Central Anatolian deciduous forests	Turkey
Central China loess plateau mixed forests	China
Central European mixed forests	Austria Belarus, Czech Republic Germany Lithuania Moldova Poland
Central Korean deciduous forests	North Korea South Korea

Changbai Mountains mixed forests	China North Korea
Changjiang Plain evergreen forests	China
Crimean Submediterranean forest complex	Russia Ukraine
Daba Mountains evergreen forests	China
Dinaric Mountains mixed forests	Albania Bosnia and Herzegovina Croatia Italy Montenegro Serbia Slovenia
East European forest steppe	Bulgaria Moldova Romania Russia Ukraine
Eastern Anatolian deciduous forests	Turkey
English Lowlands beech forests	United Kingdom
Euxine-Colchic deciduous forests	Georgia Turkey
Hokkaido deciduous forests	Japan
Huang He Plain mixed forests	China
Madeira evergreen forests	Portugal
Manchurian mixed forests	China North Korea Russia South Korea
Nihonkai evergreen forests	Japan
Nihonkai montane deciduous forests	Japan
North Atlantic moist mixed forests	Ireland United Kingdom

Northeast China Plain deciduous forests	China
Pannonian mixed forests	Austria Bosnia and Herzegovina Croatia, Czech Republic Hungary Romania Serbia Slovakia Slovenia Ukraine
Po Basin mixed forests	Italy
Pyrenees conifer and mixed forests	Andorra France, Spain
Qin Ling Mountains deciduous forests	China
Rodope montane mixed forests	Bulgaria Greece Macedonia Serbia
Sarmatic mixed forests	Belarus Estonia Finland Latvia Lithuania Norway Russia Sweden
Sichuan Basin evergreen broadleaf forests	China
South Sakhalin-Kurile mixed forests	Russia
Southern Korea evergreen forests	South Korea
Taiheiyo evergreen forests	Japan
Taiheiyo montane deciduous forests	Japan

Tarim Basin deciduous forests and steppe	China
Ussuri broadleaf and mixed forests	Russia
West Siberian broadleaf and mixed forests	Russia
Western European broadleaf forests	Austria Czech Republic France Germany Switzerland
Zagros Mountains forest steppe	Iran
Americas	
Nearctic Temperate Broadleaf and Mixed Forests	
Allegheny Highlands forests	United States
Appalachian mixed mesophytic forests	United States
Appalachian-Blue Ridge forests	United States
California mixed evergreen forest	United States
Central U.S. hardwood forests	United States
East Central Texas forests	United States
Eastern forest-boreal transition	Canada United States
Eastern Great Lakes lowland forests	Canada United States
Gulf of St. Lawrence lowland forests	Canada
Lac Saint-Jean and Saguenay valley forests	Canada
Mississippi lowland forests	United States
New England-Acadian forests	Canada United States
Northeastern coastal forests	United States
Ozark Mountain forests	United States
Southeastern mixed forests	United States
Southern Great Lakes forests	United States

Upper Midwest forest-savanna transition	United States
Western Great Lakes forests	Canada United States
Willamette Valley forests	United States
Neotropic Temperate Broadleaf and Mixed Forests	
Juan Fernandez Islands temperate forests	Chile
Magellanic subpolar forests	Argentina Chile
San Felix-San Ambrosio Islands temperate forests (Desventuradas Islands)	Chile
Valdivian temperate rain forests	Argentina Chile

7 Tropical Dry Broadleaf Forest Biome

Tropical Broadleaf Dry Forest

The tropical and subtropical dry broadleaf forest biome, also known as tropical dry forest, is located at tropical and subtropical latitudes. Though these forests occur in climates that are warm year-round, and may receive several hundred centimetres of rain per year, they have long dry seasons which last several months and vary with geographic location. These seasonal droughts have great impact on all living things in the forest.

Deciduous trees predominate in most of these forests, and during the drought a leafless period occurs, which varies with species type. Because trees lose moisture through their leaves, the shedding of leaves allows trees such as teak and mountain ebony to conserve water during dry periods.

The newly bare trees open up the canopy layer, enabling sunlight to reach ground level and facilitate the growth of thick underbrush. Trees on moister sites and those with access to ground water tend to be evergreen. Infertile sites also tend to support evergreen trees.

Three tropical dry broadleaf forest ecoregions, the East Deccan dry evergreen forests, the Sri Lanka dry-zone dry evergreen forests, and the Southeastern Indochina dry evergreen forests, are characterized by evergreen trees.

Though less biologically diverse than rainforests, tropical dry forests are home to a wide variety of wildlife including monkeys, deer, large cats, parrots, various rodents, and ground dwelling birds. Mammalian biomass tends to be higher in dry forests than in rain forests, especially in Asian and African dry forests. Many of these species display extraordinary adaptations to the difficult climate.

This biome is alternately known as the tropical and subtropical dry forest biome or the tropical and subtropical deciduous forest biome. Locally some of these forests are also called monsoon forests, and they tend to merge into savannas.

Geographical Variation

Dry forests tend to exist north and south of the equator rain forest belt, south or north of the subtropical deserts, generally in two bands, one between 10° and 20°N latitude and the other between 20° and 30°S latitude.

The most diverse dry forests in the world occur in southern Mexico and in the Bolivian lowlands. The dry forests of the Pacific Coast of northwestern South America support a wealth of unique species due to their dry climate. The subtropical forests of Maputo land-Ponderousin the subtropical regions of the United States of America and in southeastern Africa are diverse and support many endemic species.

The dry forests of central India and Indochina are notable for their diverse large vertebrate faunas. Madagascar dry deciduous forests and New Caledonia dry forests are also highly distinctive (pronounced extremism and a large number of reliquary taxa) for a wide range of taxa and at higher taxonomic levels. Trees use underground water during the dry seasons.

Biodiversity Patterns and Requirements

Species tend to have wider ranges than moist forest species, although in some regions many species do display highly restricted ranges; most dry forest species are restricted to tropical dry forests, particularly in plants; beta diversity and alpha diversity high but typically lower than adjacent moist forests.

Effective conservation of dry broadleaf forests requires the preservation of large and continuous areas of forest. Large natural areas are required to maintain larger predators and other vertebrates, and to buffer sensitive species from hunting pressure. The persistence of riparian forests and water sources is critical for many dry forest species. Large swathes of intact forest are required to allow species to recover from occasional large events, like forest fires.

Dry forests are highly sensitive to excessive burning and deforestation; overgrazing and exotic species can also quickly alter natural communities; restoration is possible but challenging, particularly if degradation has been intense and persistent. Degrading dry broadleaf often leaves thorny shrublands, thickets, or dry grasslands in their place.

Tropical Moist Broadleaf Forests

Tropical and subtropical moist broadleaf forests (TSMF), also known as tropical moist forests, are a tropical and subtropical forest biome.

Tropical and subtropical forest regions with lower rainfall are home to tropical and subtropical dry broadleaf forests and tropical and subtropical coniferous forests. Temperate rain forests also occur in certain humid temperate coastal regions.

The biome includes several types of forests:

- Lowland equatorial evergreen rain forests, commonly known as tropical rainforests, are forests which receive high rainfall (more than 2000 mm, or 80 inches, annually) throughout the year. These forests occur in a belt around the equator, with the largest areas in the Amazon basin of South America, the Congo basin of central Africa, Indonesia, and New Guinea.
- Moist deciduous and semi-evergreen seasonal forests, receive high overall rainfall with a warm summer wet

season and a cooler winter dry season. Some trees in these forests drop some or all of their leaves during the winter dry season. These forests are found in parts of South America, in Central America and around the Caribbean, in coastal West Africa, parts of the Indian subcontinent, and across much of Indochina.

- Montane rain forests, some of which are known as cloud forests, are found in cooler-climate mountainous areas.
- Flooded forests, including freshwater swamp forests and peat swamp forests.

Tropical and subtropical moist broadleaf forests are common in several terrestrial ecozones, including parts of the Afrotropic (equatorial Africa), Indomalaya (parts of the Indian subcontinent and Southeast Asia), the Neotropic (northern South America and Central America), Australasia (eastern Indonesia, New Guinea, northern and eastern Australia), and Oceania (the tropical islands of the Pacific Ocean). About half of the world's tropical rainforests are in the South American countries cf Brazil and Peru. Rainforests now cover less than 6 per cent of Earth's land surface. Scientists estimate that more than half of all the world's plant and animal species live in tropical rain forests.

Kelp Forest Biome

Kelp forests are underwater areas with a high density of kelp. They are recognized as one of the most productive and dynamic ecosystems on Earth. Smaller areas of anchored kelp are called kelp beds.

Kelp forests occur worldwide throughout temperate and polar coastal oceans. In 2007, kelp forests were also discovered in tropical waters near Ecuador.

Physically formed by brown macroalgae of the order Laminariales, kelp forests provide a unique three-dimensional habitat for marine organisms and are a source for understanding many ecological processes. Over the last century, they have been the focus of extensive research, particularly in trophic ecology, and continue to provoke important ideas that are relevant beyond this unique ecosystem. For example, kelp forests can influence coastal oceanographic patterns and provide many ecosystem services.

However, the influence of humans has often contributed to kelp forest degradation. Of particular concern are the effects of overfishing nearshore ecosystems, which can release herbivores from their normal population regulation and result in the over-grazing of kelp and other algae. This can rapidly result in transitions to barren landscapes where relatively few species persist. The implementation of marine protected areas (MPAs) is one management strategy useful for addressing such issues since it may limit the impacts of fishing and buffer the ecosystem from additive effects of other environmental stressors.

Kelp

The term 'kelp' refers to marine algae belonging to the taxonomic order Laminariales (Phylum: Heterokontophyta). Though not considered a taxonomically diverse order, kelps are highly diverse structurally and functionally. The most widely recognized species are the giant kelps (*Macrocystis spp.*), although there are numerous other genera such as *Laminaria*, *Ecklonia*, *Lessonia*, *Alaria* and *Eisenia*.

Frequently considered an ecosystem engineer, kelp provides a physical substrate and habitat for kelp forest communities. In algae (Kingdom: Protista), the body of an individual organism is known as a thallus rather than as a plant (Kingdom: Plantae). The morphological structure of a kelp thallus is defined by three basic structural units:

1. The holdfast is a root-like mass that anchors the thallus to the sea floor, though unlike true roots it is not responsible for absorbing and delivering nutrients to the rest of the thallus.
2. The stipe is analogous to a plant stalk, extending vertically from the holdfast and providing a support framework for other morphological features.
3. The fronds are leaf- or blade-like attachments extending from the stipe, sometimes along its full length, and are the sites of nutrient uptake and photosynthetic activity.

In addition, many kelp species have pneumatocysts, or gas-filled bladders, usually located at the base of fronds near the stipe. Those structures provide the necessary buoyancy for kelp to maintain an upright position in the water column.

The environmental factors necessary for kelp to survive include hard substrate (usually rock), high nutrients (e.g., nitrogen, phosphorus), and light (minimum annual irradiance dose > 50 E m^{-2}). Especially productive kelp forests tend to be associated with areas of significant oceanographic upwelling, a process that delivers cool nutrient-rich water from depth to the ocean's mixed surface layer. Water flow and turbulence facilitate nutrient assimilation across kelp fronds throughout the water column. Water clarity affects the depth to which sufficient light can be transmitted. In ideal conditions, giant kelp (*Macrocystis spp.*) can grow as much as 30-60 centimetres vertically per day. Some species such as *Nereocystis* are annual while others like *Eisenia* are perennial, living for more than 20 years. In perennial kelp forests, maximum growth rates occur during upwelling months (typically spring and summer) and die-backs correspond to reduced nutrient availability, shorter photoperiods and increased storm frequency.

Kelps are primarily associated with temperate and arctic waters worldwide. Of the more dominant species, *Laminaria* is mainly associated with both sides of the Atlantic Ocean and the coasts of China and Japan; *Ecklonia* is found in Australia, New Zealand, and South Africa; and *Macrocystis* occurs throughout the northeastern and southeastern Pacific Ocean, Southern Ocean archipelagos, and in patches around Australia, New Zealand and South Africa. The region with the greatest diversity of kelps (>20 species) is the northeastern Pacific, from north of San Francisco, California, to the Aleutian Islands, Alaska.

Although kelp forests are unknown in tropical surface waters, a few species of *Laminaria* have been known to occur exclusively in tropical deep waters. This general absence of kelp from the tropics is believed to be mostly due to insufficient nutrient levels associated with warm, oligotrophic waters. One recent study spatially overlaid the requisite physical parametres for kelp with mean oceanographic conditions has produced a model predicting the existence of subsurface kelps throughout the tropics worldwide to depths of 200 m. For a hotspot in the Galapagos Islands, the local model was improved with fine-scale data and tested; the research team found thriving kelp forests in all 8 of their sampled sites, all of which had been predicted by the model and thus validated their approach. This suggests that their global model might actually be fairly accurate and if so, kelp forests would be prolific in tropical subsurface waters worldwide. The importance of this contribution has been rapidly acknowledged within the scientific community and prompts an entirely new trajectory of kelp forest research, particularly emphasizing the potential for a spatial refuge from climate change and explanations to evolutionary patterns of kelps worldwide.

The Architecture of a Kelp Forest Ecosystem

The architecture of a kelp forest ecosystem is based on its physical structure, which influences the associated species that define its community structure. Structurally, the ecosystem includes three guilds of kelp and two guilds occupied by other algae:

- *Canopy* kelps include the largest species and often constitute floating canopies that extend to the ocean surface (e.g., *Macrocystis* and *Alaria*).
- *Stipitate* kelps generally extend a few metres above the sea floor and can grow in dense aggregations (e.g., *Eisenia* and *Ecklonia*).
- *Prostrate* kelps lie near and along the sea floor (e.g., *Laminaria*).
- The *benthic assemblage* is composed of other algal species (e.g., filamentous and foliose functional groups, articulated corallines) and sessile organisms along the ocean bottom.
- *Encrusting* coralline algae directly and often extensively cover geologic substrate.

Multiple Kelp Species

Multiple kelp species often co-exist within a forest; the term *understory canopy* refers to the stipitate and prostrate kelps. For example, a *Macrocystis* canopy may extend many metres above the seafloor towards the ocean surface, while an understory of the kelps *Eisenia* and *Pterygophora* reaches upward only a few metres. Beneath these kelps there may be a benthic assemblage of foliose red algae. The dense vertical infrastructure with overlying canopy forms a system of microenvironments similar to those observed in a terrestrial forest, with a sunny canopy region, a partially shaded middle, and darkened seafloor. Each guild has associated organisms, which vary in their levels of dependence on the habitat, and the assemblage of these organisms can vary with kelp morphologies. For example, in California *Macrocystis pyrifera* forests, the nudibranch *Melibe leonina* and skeleton shrimp *Caprella californica* are closely associated with surface canopies; the kelp perch *Brachyistius frenatus*, rockfish *Sebastes spp.* and many other fishes are found within the stipitate understory; brittle stars and turban snails *Tegula spp.* are closely associated with the kelp holdfast, while various herbivores such as sea urchins and abalone live under the prostrate canopy; many seastars, hydroids and benthic fishes live among the benthic assemblages; solitary corals, various gastropods and echinoderms live over the encrusting coralline algae. In addition, pelagic fishes and marine mammals are loosely associated with kelp forests, usually interacting near the edges as they visit to feed on resident organisms.

Trophic Ecology

Classic studies in kelp forest ecology have largely focused on trophic interactions (the relationships between organisms and their food webs), particularly the understanding and top-down trophic processes. Bottom-up processes are generally driven by the abiotic conditions required for primary producers to grow, such as availability of light and nutrients, and the subsequent transfer of energy to consumers at higher trophic levels. For example, the occurrence of kelp is frequently correlated with oceanographic upwelling zones, which provide unusually high concentrations of nutrients to the local environment. This allows kelp to grow and subsequently support herbivores, which in turn support consumers at higher trophic levels. By contrast, in top-down processes, predators limit the biomass of species at lower trophic levels through consumption. In the absence of predation, these lower level species flourish because resources that support their energetic requirements are non-limiting. In a well-studied example from Alaskan kelp forests, sea otters (*Enhydra lutris*) control populations of herbivorous sea urchins through predation. When sea otters are removed from the ecosystem (for example, by human exploitation), urchin populations are released from predatory control and grow dramatically. This leads to increased herbivore pressure on local kelp stands. Deterioration of the kelp itself results in the loss of physical ecosystem structure and subsequently, the loss of other species associated with this habitat. In Alaskan kelp forest ecosystems, sea otters are the keystone species that mediates this trophic cascade. In Southern California, kelp forests persist without sea otters and the control of herbivorous urchins is instead mediated by a suite of predators including lobsters and large fishes. The effect of removing one predatory species in this system differs from Alaska because there is redundancy in the trophic levels and other predatory species can continue to regulate urchins. However, the removal of multiple predators can effectively release urchins from predator pressure and allow the system to follow trajectories towards kelp forest degradation. Similar examples exist in Nova Scotia, South Africa, Australia and Chile. The relative importance of top-down versus bottom-up control in kelp forest ecosystems and the strengths of trophic interactions continue to be the subject of considerable scientific investigation.

The transition from macroalgal (i.e. kelp forest) to denuded landscapes dominated by sea urchins (or 'urchin barrens') is a widespread phenomenon, often resulting from trophic cascades like those described above; the two phases are regarded as alternative stable states of the ecosystem. The recovery of kelp forests from barren states has been documented following dramatic perturbations, such as urchin disease or large shifts in thermal conditions. Recovery from intermediate states of deterioration is less predictable and depends on a combination of abiotic factors and biotic interactions in each case.

Though urchins are usually the dominant herbivore, others with significant interaction strengths include seastars, isopods, kelp crabs, and herbivorous fishes. In many cases, these organisms feed on kelp that has been dislodged from substrate and drifts near the ocean floor rather than expend energy searching for intact thalli to feed on. When there is sufficient drift kelp, herbivorous grazers do not exert pressure on attached plants; when drift subsidies are unavailable, grazers directly impact the physical structure of the ecosystem. Many studies in Southern California have demonstrated that the availability of drift kelp specifically influences the foraging behaviour of sea urchins. Drift kelp and kelp-derived particulate matter have also been important in subsidizing adjacent habitats, such as sandy beaches and the rocky intertidal.

Patches

Another major area of kelp forest research has been directed at understanding the spatial-temporal patterns of kelp patches. Not only do such dynamics affect the physical landscape, but they also affect species that associate with kelp for refuge or foraging activities. Large-scale environmental disturbances have offered important insights concerning mechanisms and ecosystem resilience. Examples of environmental disturbances include the following:

- *Acute and chronic pollution* events have been shown to impact southern California kelp forests, though the intensity of the impact seems to depend on both the nature of the contaminants and duration of exposure. Pollution can include sediment deposition and eutrophication from sewage, industrial byproducts and contaminants like PCBs and heavy metals (for example, copper, zinc), runoff of organophosphates from agricultural areas, anti-fouling chemicals used in harbors and marinas (for example, TBT and creosote) and land-based pathogens like fecal coliform bacteria.

- *Catastrophic storms* can remove surface kelp canopies through wave activity but usually leave understory kelps intact; they can also remove urchins when little spatial refuge is available. Interspersed canopy clearings create a seascape mosaic where sunlight penetrates deeper into the kelp forest and species that are normally light-limited in the understory can flourish. Similarly, substrate cleared of kelp holdfasts can provide space for other sessile species to establish themselves and occupy the seafloor, sometimes directly competing with juvenile kelp and even inhibiting their settlement.
- *El Niño-Southern Oscillation* (*ENSO*) events involve the depression of oceanographic thermoclines, severe reductions of nutrient input, and changes in storm patterns. Stress due to warm water and nutrient depletion can increase the susceptibility of kelp to storm damage and herbivorous grazing, sometimes even prompting phase shifts to urchin-dominated landscapes. In general, oceanographic conditions (that is, water temperature, currents) influence the recruitment success of kelp and its competitors, which clearly affect subsequent species interactions and kelp forest dynamics.
- *Overfishing* higher trophic levels that naturally regulate herbivore populations is also recognized as an important stressor in kelp forests. As described in the previous section, the drivers and outcomes of trophic cascades are important for understanding spatial-temporal patterns of kelp forests.

In addition to ecological monitoring of kelp forests before, during, and after such disturbances, scientists try to tease apart the intricacies of kelp forest dynamics using experimental manipulations. By working on smaller spatial-temporal scales, they can control for the presence or absence of specific biotic and abiotic factors to discover the operative mechanisms. For example, in southern Australia, manipulations of kelp canopy types demonstrated that the relative amount of *Ecklonia radiata* in a canopy could be used to predict understory species assemblages; consequently, the proportion of *E. radiata* can be used as an indicator of other species occurring in the environment.

Human Use

Kelp forests have been important to human existence for thousands of years. Indeed, many now theorise that the first colonisation of the Americas was due to fishing communities following the Pacific Kelp Forests during the last Ice Age. One theory contends that the kelp forests that would have stretched from northeast Asia to the American Pacific coast would have provided many benefits to ancient boaters. The kelp forests would have provided many sustenance opportunities as well as acting as a type of buffer from rough water. Besides these benefits researchers believe that the kelp forests might have helped early boaters navigate, acting as a type of 'kelp highway'. Theorists also suggest that the kelp forests would have helped these ancient colonists by providing a stable way of life and preventing them from having to adapt to new ecosystems and develop new survival methods even as they traveled thousands of miles.

Modern economies are based on fisheries of kelp-associated species like lobster and rockfish. Humans also harvest kelp directly to feed aquaculture species like abalone and to extract the compound alginic acid, which is used in products like toothpaste and antacids. Kelp forests are valued for recreational activities such as SCUBA diving and kayaking; the industries that support these sports represent one benefit related to the ecosystem and the enjoyment derived from these activities represents another. All of these are examples of ecosystem services provided specifically by kelp forests.

Threats and Management

Given the complexity of kelp forests – their variable structure, geography and interactions – they pose a considerable challenge to environmental managers. It is difficult to extrapolate even well-studied trends to the future because interactions within the ecosystem will change under variable conditions, not all relationships in the ecosystem are understood, and there can be non-linear thresholds to transitions that are not yet recognized. With respect to kelp forests, major issues of concern include marine pollution and water quality, kelp harvesting and fisheries, invasive species and climate change. It has been argued that the most pressing threat to kelp forest preservation is the overfishing of coastal ecosystems, which by removing higher trophic levels facilitates their shift to depauperate urchin barrens. The maintenance of biodiversity is recognized as a way of generally stabilizing ecosystems and their services through mechanisms such as functional compensation and reduced susceptibility to foreign species invasions.

In many places, managers have opted to regulate the harvest of kelp and/or the taking of kelp forest species by fisheries. While these may be effective in one sense, they do not necessarily protect the entirety of the ecosystem. Marine protected areas (MPAs) offer a unique solution that encompasses not only target species for harvesting but also the interactions surrounding them and the local environment as a whole. Direct benefits of MPAs to fisheries (for example, spillover effects) have been well documented around the world.

Indirect benefits have also been shown for several cases among species such as abalone and fishes in Central California. Most importantly, studies have demonstrated that MPAs can be effective at protecting existing kelp forest ecosystems and may also allow for the regeneration of those that have been impacted.

9 Red Forest Biome

Worm Wood Forest

The Red Forest, formerly the Worm Wood Forest, refers to the trees in the 10 km² surrounding the Chernobyl Nuclear Power Plant. The name 'Red Forest' comes from the ginger-brown colour of the pine trees after they died following the absorption of high levels of radiation from the Chernobyl accident on April 26, 1986. In the post-disaster cleanup operations, the Red Forest was bulldozed and buried in 'waste graveyards'. The site of the Red Forest remains one of the most contaminated areas in the world today.

The Red Forest is located in the zone of alienation; this area received the highest doses of radiation from the Chernobyl accident and the resulting clouds of smoke and dust, heavily polluted with radiation. The trees died from this radiation. The explosion and fire at the Chernobyl No. 4 reactor contaminated the soil, water and atmosphere with the radiation equivalent to 20 times of the atomic bombings of Hiroshima and Nagasaki.

In the post-disaster cleanup operations, a majority of the pine trees were bulldozed and buried in trenches by the 'liquidators'. The trenches were then covered with a thick carpet of sand and planted with pine saplings. Many fear that as the trees decay, radiation will leach into the ground water. People have evacuated the contaminated zone around the Red Forest.

Flora and Fauna of the Red Forest

As humans were evacuated from the area in 1986, animals moved in despite the radiation. The flora and fauna of the Red Forest have been dramatically affected by the radioactive contamination that followed the accident. It seems that the biodiversity of the Red Forest has increased in the years following the disaster. There are reports of some stunted plants in the area. Wild boar have multiplied eightfold between 1986 and 1988.

The site of the Red Forest remains one of the most contaminated areas in the world. However, it has proved to be an astonishingly fertile habitat for many endangered species. The evacuation of the area surrounding the nuclear reactor has created a lush and unique wildlife refuge. In the 1996 BBC *Horizon* documentary 'Inside Chernobyl's Sarcophagus', birds are seen flying in and out of large holes in the structure of the former nuclear reactor. The long-term impact of the fallout on the flora and fauna of the region is not fully known, as plants and animals have significantly different and varying radiologic tolerance. Some birds are reported with stunted tail feathers (which interferes with breeding). Storks, wolves, beavers, and eagles have been reported in the area.

Radiation Levels in the Red Forest

Today, radiation levels in the Red Forest can be as high as one röntgen per hour, but levels of ten milliröntgens per hour are more common. More than 90 per cent of the radioactivity of the Red Forest is concentrated in the soil.

Scientists are planning to use the nearby, radioactive and abandoned town of Pripyat and surrounding area as a unique laboratory for modeling the dispersal of radionuclides by the detonation of a dirty bomb or an attack with chemical or biological agents. The area offers an unparalleled opportunity to fully understand the passage of radioactive debris through an urban and rural area.

The nature of the area seems to have not only survived, but flourished due to significant reduction of human impact. The zone has become a 'Radiological Reserve', a classic example of an involuntary park. There were thought to be cases of mutant deformity in animals of the Red Forest, but none have been proven, except partial albinism in swallows. Currently, there is concern about contamination of the soil with Strontium-90 and Caesium-137, which have half-lives of about 30 years. The highest levels of Caesium-137 are found in the surface layers of the soil where they are absorbed by plants, and insects living there today. Some scientists fear that radioactivity will affect the land for the next several generations.

Fog or Cloud Forest

The fog forest, is a generally tropical or subtropical evergreen montane moist forest characterized by a persistent, frequent or seasonal low-level cloud cover, usually at the canopy level. Cloud forests often exhibit an abundance of mosses covering the ground and vegetation, in which case they are also referred to as mossy forests. Mossy forests usually develop on the saddles of mountains, where moisture introduced by settling clouds is more effectively retained.

Distribution and Climate of Fog Forest

Dependent on local climate, which is affected by the distance to the sea, the exposition and the latitude, the altitude varies from 500 m to 4000 m above sea level. Typically, there is a relatively small band of altitude in which the atmospheric environment is suitable for cloud forest development. This is characterized by persistent mist or clouds at the vegetation level, resulting in the reduction of direct sunlight and thus of evapotranspiration. Within cloud forests, much of the precipitation is in the form of fog drip, where fog condenses on tree leaves and then drips onto the ground below.

Tropical cloud forests extend from 23°N to 25°S latitudes and occur in a relatively narrow altitudinal zone with a special atmospheric environment which is characterized by at the vegetation level. Annual rainfall can range from 500 to 10,000 mm/year and mean temperature between 8 to 20° C.

While cloud forest today is the most widely used term, in some regions these ecosystems or special types of cloud forests are called mossy forest, elfin forest, montane thicket, dwarf cloud forest, nuboselva, bosque montano nebuloso, selva de neblina, bosque nuboso, bosque de ceja, selva sublada, nebelwald, wolkenwald, forêt néphéliphile, forêt de nuage, unmu-rin, bosque anao, foresta nebular, mata nebular, matinha nebular, floresta fe neblina, floresta nuvigena, mata de neblina, matinha de altitude, floresta nublada, and floresta pluvial montana e/ou alto montana.

The definition of cloud forest can be ambiguous, with many countries not using the term (preferring such terms as Afromontane forest and upper montane rain forest, montane laurel forest, or more localised terms such as the Bolivian yungas, and the laurisilva of the Atlantic Islands), and occasionally subtropical and even temperate forests in which similar meteorological conditions occur are considered to be cloud forests.

Only one per cent of the global woodland is covered by cloud forests.

Important areas of cloud forest are in Central and South America, East and Central Africa, Indonesia, Malaysia, at the Philippines, Papua-New Guinea and in the Caribbean.

Temperate Cloud Forests and Their Distribution

Although far from being universally accepted as true cloud forests, several forests in temperate regions have strong similarities with tropical cloud forests. The term is further confused by occasional reference to cloud forests in tropical countries as 'temperate' due to the cooler climate associated with these misty forests.

Distribution of Temperate Cloud Forests

- Argentina - Catamarca and Tucumán
- Australia - Lamington National Park (Queensland)

- Chile (Bosque de Fray Jorge National Park)
- People's Republic of China - Yunnan Plateau, mountains of southern and eastern China
- Japan - parts of Yakushima Island
- New Zealand - parts of Fiordland, Mount Taranaki and Mount Cargill, near Dunedin.
- Portugal - Azores and Madeira
- South Africa
- Spain - Canary Islands (laurisilva)
- Taiwan - Chiantianshan Nature Reserve, Yuanyang Lake Nature Reserve
- United States - Redwood Coast

Characteristics

In comparison with lower tropical moist forests, cloud forests show a reduced tree stature combined with increased stem density and generally the lower diversity of woody plants. Trees in these regions are generally shorter and more heavily stemmed than in lower altitude forests in the same regions, often with gnarled trunks and branches, forming dense, compact crowns. Their leaves become smaller, thicker and harder with increasing altitude. The high moisture promotes the development of a high biomass and biodiversity of epiphyte, particularly bryophytes, lichens, ferns (including filmy ferns), bromeliads and orchids. The number of endemic plants can be very high.

An important feature of cloud forests is that the tree crowns can intercept the wind-driven cloud moisture, part of which drips to the ground. This water stripped from the clouds is termed horizontal or occult (because it is not recorded with normal rainfall measurement) precipitation, and can be an important contribution to the hydrologic cycle.

Due to the high water content of the soil, the reduced solar radiation and the low rates of decomposition and mineralization, the soil acidity is very high, with more humus and peat often forming the upper soil layer.

Researcher distinguishes two general types of tropical montane cloud forests:

- Areas with a high annual precipitation due to a frequent cloud cover in combination with heavy and sometimes persistent orographic rainfall; such forests have a perceptible canopy strata, a high number of epiphytes and a thick peat layer which has a high storage capacity for water and control the runoff.
- In drier areas with mainly seasonal rainfall cloud stripping can amount to a large proportion of the annual precipitation.

Importance of Cloud Forests

- *Watershed function:* Because of the cloud stripping strategy the effective rainfall can be doubled in dry seasons and increase the wet season rainfall by about 10 per cent. Experiments of researcher showed that the tree canopies of non-cloud forests intercept and evaporate 20 per cent more of the precipitation than cloud forests, which means a loss to the land component of the hydrological cycle.
- *Vegetation:* Tropical montane cloud forests are not as species-rich as tropical lowland forests but they provide the habitats for many species that are found nowhere else For example, the Cerro de la Neblina, a cloud covered mountain in the south of Venezuela accommodates many shrubs, orchids and insectivorous plants which are restricted to this mountain only.
- *Fauna:* The endemism in animals is also very high. In Peru, more than one third of the 270 endemic birds, mammals and frogs are found in cloud forests. One of the best known cloud forest mammal is the Mountain Gorilla (*Gorilla b. beringei*). Many of those endemic animals have important functions such as seed dispersal and forest dynamics in this ecosystems.

In 1970, the original extent of cloud forests was around 50 million hectares. Population growth, poverty and uncontrolled land use have contributed to the loss of cloud forests. The 1990 Global Forest Survey found that 1.1 per cent of tropical mountain and highland forests were lost each year, which was higher than in any other tropical forests. In Colombia, one of the countries with the largest area of cloud forests, only 10-20 per cent of the initial cloud forest cover remains. Significant areas have been converted to plantations, or for use in agriculture and pasture. Important crops in montane forest zones are tea and coffee, but also logging special species such as Podocarpus causes changes to forest structure.

Currently, one third of all cloud forests are protected.

Impact of Climate Change on Cloud Forests

Because of their delicate dependency on local climate, cloud forests will be strongly affected by global climate change. A number of climate models suggest that the low-altitude cloudiness will be reduced, which means that the optimum climate for many cloud forest habitats will increase in altitude. Linked to the reduction of cloud moisture immersion and increasing temperature, the hydrological cycle will change with the consequence that the system will dry out.

This can result in the wilting and the death of epiphytes, which rely on high humidity. Frogs and lizards are expected to suffer from increased drought. In addition, climate changes can result in a higher amount of hurricanes, which may increase damage to tropical montane cloud forests. All in all the results of the climate change will be a loss in biodiversity, altitude shifts in species ranges and community reshuffling and, in some areas, complete loss of cloud forests.

Forest Animals List

There are many animals that live in the forest and one can find species that are never seen in a zoo. The animals and birds live in their natural environment and some of them fall under the endangered species list due to indiscriminate hunting and poaching. Most of the animals found on earth are wild animals whose natural habitat is the forest. All animals however do not live in the same type of forests, some live exclusively in rainforests while others are found in deciduous forests, temperate hardwood forest, boreal or taiga forests and tropical dry forests. Here we will give you a list of forest animals.

Forest Animals List

Here is a list of animals that are found in a forest:

- Leopard
- African lion
- Orangutan
- Cape buffalo
- Crocodile
- Rainbow lizard
- Flying squirrel
- Giant panda
- Baboon
- Fox
- Bongo
- Bontebok
- Cheetah
- Zebra
- Fossa
- Forest hog
- Giraffe
- Gerbil

- Hare
- Hedgehog
- Jackal
- Mandrill
- Nyala
- Meerkats
- Oribi
- Otter
- Mongoose
- Seal
- Reedbuck
- Servil
- Warthog
- Waterbuck
- Wild Cat
- Badger
- Hyena
- Jaguar
- Gorilla
- Dwarf mongoose
- Lemur
- Iguana
- Monkey
- Golden toad
- Giant armadillo
- Sloth
- Squirrel monkey
- Pygmy marmoset
- Elephant
- Aye-Aye monkey
- Bengal tiger
- Capuchin monkey
- Poison arrow frog
- Alpaca anteater
- Ocelot
- Red deer
- Tamarin lion
- Woolly monkey
- Spider monkey
- Porcupine
- White faced monkey
- Howler monkey
- Capybara
- Okapi
- Sumatran rhinoceros
- Silvery gibbon
- Giant river otter
- Toucan
- Poison arrow frog
- Happy face spider
- Glass frog
- Skink
- Leaf-Cutter ant
- Bush pig
- Strawberry poisoned dart frog
- Addax
- Antelope

Endangered Forest Animals List

Here is an endangered forest animals list:

- Bactrian camel
- Bahamas rock iguana

- Bale monkey
- Owl faced monkey
- Ostrich
- Ouachita burrowing crayfish
- Geometric tortoise
- Galapagos land snail
- Salta toad
- Saltwater crocodile
- Samoan tree snail
- Samoan flying fox
- Sambar deer
- Salvin's salamamder
- San Diego fairy shrimp
- Uzungwe toad
- Utah prairie dog
- Usambara banana frog
- Zug's robber frog
- Zhou's box turtle
- Zapahuira water frog
- Zambian mole rat
- Zacate blanco treefrog
- Yunnan flying frog
- Yiwu salamander
- Yellowtail flounder
- Yellow-tailed woolly monkey
- Yellow-spotted salamander
- Yellow-margined box turtle
- Yellow-legged climbing salamander
- White-lipped deer
- Yellow river frog
- Yarey robber frog
- Warty Asian tree toad
- Visayan deer
- Visayan warty pig
- Volcan tacana toad
- Yamur lake grunter
- Yalobusha riverlet crayfish
- Western bearded pig
- Yap flying fox
- Wyoming toad
- Volcano rabbit
- Wrinkled madagascar frog
- Wutai crab
- Wreathed cactus snail
- Wood turtle
- Wolverine
- Wondiwoi tree kangaroo
- Wild goat
- Whitehead's spiny rat
- White-tipped tuft-tailed rat
- White-tailed mouse
- White-cheeked spider monkey
- Water frog wang's crab
- Wild yak white-tailed deer
- White-spotted madagascar frog
- Visayan warty pig
- Vietnam crocodile newt

- Vanikoro flying fox
- Unicoloured oldfield mouse
- Ubatuba dwarf frog
- Turkana mud turtle
- Tufted deer
- Tulotoma snail
- Tumbala climbing rat
- Tufted gray langur
- Tufted ground squirrel
- Tree hole crab
- Travancore flying squirrel
- Toothless blindcat timor
- Yellow tiger
- Tiger chameleon
- Tiger tail seahorse
- Telescope hornsnail
- Tibetan antelope
- Three-striped roof turtle
- Thomas's Langur
- Tennessee pebblesnail
- Tehuantepec jack rabbit
- Swamp deer
- Painted tree rat
- Palau flying fox
- Pacific pond turtle
- La palma giant lizard
- Kinabalu Asian toad
- Juliana's golden mole
- Jagged-shelled turtle
- Ivory coast frog
- Indian giant squirrel
- Sulcata tortoise
- Dhole
- Gazelle
- Florida panther
- Gray wolf
- Grizzly bear
- Koala bears
- Kinkajou
- Kangaroo rat
- Lynx
- Numbat
- Oryx
- Okapi
- Snow leopard
- Siberian tiger
- Red wolf
- Tasmanian devil
- White rhinoceros
- Wallaby
- Yak
- Zorro

Forest Birds List

Here is a list of birds that are found in the forest:

- White pelican
- Great blue heron
- Snowy egret
- Green heron
- Greater white-fronted goose
- Purple martin
- Violet-green swallow
- Wood duck
- Golden eagle
- Red-shouldered hawk

- Mountain bluebird
- Ruby-crowned kinglet
- Prairie falcon
- Black-headed heron
- Hooded vulture
- Swallow-Tailed kite
- Paradise tanager
- Long-Tailed sylph
- Black-Backed grosbeak
- Great Horned owl
- Hoopoe malachite
- Sunbird
- Scarlet macaw
- Orange winged parrot
- Woodpecker
- Belted kingfisher
- Hooded oriole
- Western meadowlark
- Hummingbird
- White-Throated swift
- Northern pygmy owl
- Yellow billed cuckoo
- Sandpiper
- Mockingbird

Endangered Forest Bird List

Here is an endangered birds list:

- Zamboanga bulbul
- Wilson's Bird-of-paradise
- Yemen thrush
- Wrinkled hornbill
- Yellowish imperial pigeon
- Northern spotted owl
- Yellow-throated hanging-parrot
- Wood stork
- Yellow-shouldered blackbird
- Prairie chicken
- Lilian's lovebird
- Yellow-legged pigeon
- White-winged collared dove
- Yellow-eyed starling
- Western spotted owl
- Marbled murrelet
- Yellow-crowned parakeet
- Kakapo
- Yellow-Crested cockatoo
- Hawaiian goose
- White-winged wood duck
- Purple eagle
- Brown-winged kingfisher

This was a list of forest animals and birds. More and more animals and birds of the forest are falling under the endangered animals list due to deforestation and poaching. So we should be fully aware of the environment and do all we can to protect these forest birds and animals.

Mechanism of Grassland Biome

Grasslands are areas where the vegetation is dominated by grasses (Poaceae) and other herbaceous (non-woody) plants (forbs). However, sedge (Cyperaceae) and rush (Juncaceae) families can also be found. Grasslands occur naturally on all continents except Antarctica. In temperate latitudes, such as northwestern Europe and the Great Plains and California in North America, native grasslands are dominated by perennial bunch grass species, whereas in warmer climates annual species form a greater component of the vegetation.

Grasslands are found in most ecological regions of the Earth. For example there are five terrestrial ecoregion classifications (subdivisions) of the temperate grasslands, savannas, and shrublands biome ('ecosystem'), which is one of eight terrestrial ecozones of the Earth's surface.

Grassland vegetation can vary in height from very short, as in chalk where the vegetation may be less than 30 cm (12 in) high, to quite tall, as in the case of North American tallgrass prairie, South American grasslands and African savanna. Woody plants, shrubs or trees, may occur on some grasslands - forming savannas, scrubby nd surface of the continent of Africa. While grasslands in general support diverse wildlife, given the lack of hiding places for predators, the African Savanna regions support a much greater diversity in wildlife than do temperate grasslands.

The appearance of mountains in the western United States during the Miocene and Pliocene epochs, a period of some 25 million years, created a continental climate favorable to the evolution of grasslands. Existing forest biomes declined, and grasslands became much more widespread. Following the Pleistocene Ice Ages, grasslands expanded in range in the hotter, drier climates, and began to become the dominant land feature worldwide.

As flowering plants, grasses grow in great concentrations in climates where annual rainfall ranges between 500 and 900 mm (20 and 35 in). The root systems of perennial grasses and forbs form complex mats that hold the soil in place. Mites, insect larvae, nematodes and earthworms inhabit deep soil, which can reach 6 metres (20 ft) underground in undisturbed grasslands on the richest soils of the world. These invertebrates, along with symbiotic fungi, extend the root systems, break apart hard soil, enrich it with urea and other natural fertilizers, trap minerals and water and promote growth. Some types of fungi make the plants more resistant to insect and microbial attacks.

Natural grasslands primarily occur in regions that receive between 250 and 900 mm (9.8 and 35 in) of rain per year, as compared with deserts, which receive less than 250 mm (9.8 in) and tropical rainforests, which receive more than 2,000 mm (79 in). Anthropogenic grasslands often occur in much higher rainfall zones, as high as 200 cm (79 in) annual rainfall. Grassland can exist naturally in areas with higher rainfall when other factors prevent the growth of forests, such as in serpentine barrens, where minerals in the soil inhibit most plants from growing.

Average daily temperatures range between –20 and 30° C. Temperate grasslands have warm summers and cold winters with rain or some snow.

Grassland Biodiversity and Conservation

Grasslands dominated by unsown wild-plant communities ('unimproved grasslands') can be called either natural or 'semi-natural' habitats. The majority of grasslands in temperate climates are 'semi-natural'. Although their plant communities are natural, their maintenance depends upon anthropogenic activities such as low-intensity farming, which maintains these grasslands through grazing and cutting regimes. These grasslands contain many species of wild plants - grasses, sedges, rushes and herbs - 25 or more speerican prairie grasslands or lowland wildflower meadows in the UK are now rare and their associated wild flora equally threatened. Associated with the wild-plant diversity of the 'unimproved' grasslands is usually a rich invertebrate fauna; also there are many species of birds that are grassland 'specialists', such as the snipe and the Great Bustard. Agriculturally improved grasslands, which dominate modern intensive agricultural landscapes, are usually poor in wild plant species due to the original diversity of plants having been destroyed by cultivation, the original wild-plant communities having been replaced by sown monocultures of cultivated varieties of grasses and clovers, such as Perennial ryegrass and White Clover. In many parts of the world 'unimproved' grasslands are one of the least threatened habitats, and a target for acquisition by wildlife conservation groups or for special grants to landowners who are encouraged to manage them appropriately.

Grasslands are of vital importance for raising livestock for human consumption and for milk and other dairy products.

Grassland vegetation remains dominant in a particular area usually due to grazing, cutting, or natural or manmade fires, all discouraging colonisation by and survival of tree and shrub seedlings. Some of the world's largest expanses of grassland are found in African savanna, and these are maintained by wild herbivores as well as by nomadic pastoralists and their cattle, sheep or goats.

Grasslands may occur naturally or as the result of human activity. Grasslands created and maintained by human activity are called anthropogenic grasslands. Hunting peoples around the world often set regular fires to maintain and extend grasslands, and prevent fire-intolerant trees and shrubs from taking hold. The tallgrass prairies in the American Midwest may have been extended eastward into Illinois, Indiana, and Ohio by human agency. Much grassland in northwest Europe developed after the Neolithic Period, when people gradually cleared the forest to create areas for raising their livestock.

Tropical and Subtropical Grasslands

These grasslands are classified with tropical and subtropical savannas and shrublands as the tropical and subtropical grasslands, savannas, and shrublands biome. Notable tropical and subtropical grasslands include the Llanos grasslands of northern South America.

Temperate Grasslands

Mid-latitude grasslands, including the Prairie and Pacific Grasslands of North America, the Pampas of Argentina, Brazil and Uruguay, calcareous downland, and the steppes of Europe. They are classified with temperate savannas and shrublands as the temperate grasslands, savannas, and shrublands biome. Temperate grasslands are the home to many large herbivores, such as bison, gazelles, zebras, rhinoceroses, and wild horses. Carnivores like lions, wolves and cheetahs and leopards are also found in temperate grasslands. Other animals of this region include: deer, prairie dogs, mice, jack rabbits, skunks, coyotes, snakes, fox, owls, badgers, blackbirds (both Old and New World varieties), grasshoppers, meadowlarks, sparrows, quails, hawks and hyenas.

Flooded Grasslands

Grasslands that are flooded seasonally or year-round, like the Everglades of Florida, the Pantanal of Brazil, Bolivia and Paraguay or the Esteros del Ibera in Argentina.They are classified with flooded savannas as the flooded grasslands and savannas biome and occur mostly in the tropics and subtropics.

Montane Grasslands

High-altitude grasslands located on high mountain ranges around the world, like the Páramo of the Andes Mountains. They are part of the montane grasslands and shrublands biome and also constitute tundra.

Tundra Grasslands

Similar to montane grasslands, polar arctic tundra can have grasses, but high soil moisture means that few tundras are grass-dominated today. However, during the Pleistocene ice ages, a polar grassland known as steppe-tundra occupied large areas of the Northern hemisphere. These are in the tundra biome.

Desert and Xeric Grasslands

Also called desert grasslands, this is composed of sparse grassland ecoregions located in the deserts and xeric shrublands biome.

Fauna

Grassland in all its form supports a vast variety of mammals, reptiles, birds, and insects. Typical large mammals include the Blue Wildebeest, American Bison, Giant Anteater and Przewalski's Horse.

There is evidence for grassland being much the product of animal behaviour and movement; some examples include migratory herds of antelope trampling vegetation and African Bush Elephants eating Acacia saplings before the plant has a chance to grow into a mature tree.

Pampas

The Pampas (from Quechua, meaning 'plain') are the fertile South American lowlands, covering more than 750,000 km^2 (289,577 sq mi), that include the Argentine provinces of Buenos Aires, La Pampa, Santa Fe, Entre Ríos and Córdoba, most of Uruguay, and the southernmost Brazilian State, Rio Grande do Sul. These vast plains are only interrupted by the low Ventana and Tandil hills near Bahía Blanca and Tandil (Argentina), with a height of 1,300 m (4,265 ft) and 500 m (1,640 ft) respectively. The climate is mild, with precipitation of 600 mm (23.6 in) to 1,200 mm (47.2 in), more or less evenly distributed through the year, making the soils appropriate for agriculture. This area is also one of the distinct physiography provinces of the larger Paraná-Paraguay Plain division. These plains contain unique wildlife because of the different terrains around it. Some of this wildlife includes the rhea, the badger, and the prairie chicken.

Vegetation

Frequent wildfires ensure that only small plants such as grasses flourish, and trees are rare. The dominant vegetation types are grassy prairie and grass steppe in which numerous species of the grass genus *Stipa* are particularly conspicuous. 'Pampas Grass' (*Cortaderia selloana*) is an iconic species of the Pampas. Vegetation typically includes perennial grasses and herbs. Different strata of grasses occur because of gradients of water availability.

The World Wildlife Fund divides the Pampa into three distinct ecoregions. The Uruguayan savanna lies east of the Uruguay River, and includes all of Uruguay and the southern portion of Brazil's state of Rio Grande do Sul. The Humid Pampas include eastern Buenos Aires Province, and southern Entre Ríos Province. The Semi-arid Pampas includes western Buenos Aires Province and adjacent portions of Santa Fe, Córdoba, and La Pampa provinces. The Pampas are bounded by the drier Argentine espinal grasslands, which form a semicircle around the north, east, and south of the Humid Pampas.

Winters are cool to mild and summers are very warm and humid. Rainfall is fairly uniform throughout the year but is a little heavier during the summer. Annual rainfall is heaviest near the coast and decreases gradually further inland. Rain during the late spring and summer usually arrives in the form of brief heavy showers and thunderstorms. More general rainfall occurs the remainder of the year as cold fronts and storm systems move through. Although cold spells during the winter often send nighttime temperatures below freezing, snow is quite rare. In most winters, a few light snowfalls occur over inland areas.

Central Argentina boasts a successful agricultural business, with crops grown on the Pampas south and west of Buenos Aires. Much of the area is also used for cattle and more recently to grow vineyards in the Buenos Aires wine region. These farming regions (i.e., modified of disturbed Pampas) are particularly susceptible to flooding during heavy rainfall.

Prairie

Prairies are considered part of the temperate grasslands, savannas, and shrublands biome by ecologists, based on similar temperate climates, moderate rainfall, and grasses, herbs, and shrubs, rather than trees, as the dominant vegetation type. Temperate grassland regions include the Pampas of Argentina, Brazil and Uruguay as well as the steppes of Eurasia.

Lands typically referred to as 'prairie' tend to be in North America. The term encompasses the area referred to as the Interior Lowlands of the United States, Canada and Mexico, which includes all of the Great Plains as well as the wetter, somewhat hillier land to the east. In the U.S., the area is constituted by most or all of the states of North Dakota, South Dakota, Nebraska, Kansas, and Oklahoma, and sizable parts of the states of Montana, Wyoming, Colorado, New Mexico, Texas, Missouri, Iowa, Illinois, Indiana, Wisconsin, and western and southern Minnesota. The Central Valley of California is also a prairie. The Canadian Prairies occupy vast areas of Manitoba, Saskatchewan, and Alberta.

The formation of the North American Prairies started with the upwelling of the Rocky Mountains. The mountains created a rain shadow that killed most of the trees.

Most prairie soil was deposited during the last glacial advance that began about 110,000 years ago. The glaciers expanding southward scraped the soil, picking up material and leveling the terrain. As the glaciers retreated about 10,000 years ago, it deposited this material in the form of till.

Tallgrass Prairie evolved over tens of thousands of years with the disturbances of grazing and fire. Native ungulates such as bison, elk, and white-tailed deer, roamed the expansive, diverse, plentiful grassland before European colonization of the Americas. For 10,000-20,000 years native people used fire annually as a tool to assist in hunting, transportation and safety. Evidence of ignition sources of fire in the tallgrass prairie are overwhelmingly human as opposed to lightning. Humans, and grazing animals, were active participants in the process of prairie formation and the establishment of the diversity of graminoid and forbs species. Fire has the effect on prairies of removing trees, clearing dead plant matter, and changing the availability of certain nutrients in the soil from the ash produced. Fire kills the vascular tissue of trees, but not prairie, as up to 75 per cent (depending on the species) of the total plant biomass is below the soil surface and will re-grow from its deep (up to 6 feet) roots. Without disturbance, trees will encroach on a grassland, cast shade, which suppresses the understory. Prairie and widely spaced Oak trees evolved to coexist in the oak savanna ecosystem.

Fertility

In spite of long recurrent droughts and occasional torrential rains, the grasslands of the Great Plains are not subject to great soil erosion. The deep, interconnected root systems of prairie grasses firmly hold the soil in place and prevent run-off of soil. When a plant dies, the fungi, bacteria and the other slowly eat the roots and leaves, returning nutrients to the soil.

These deep roots also help prairie plants to reach water in even the driest conditions. The grass suffers much less damage from dry conditions than the farm crops that have replaced many former prairies.

Types

The types of prairies in North America are usually split into three groups: wet, mesic, and dry.

Wet

In this type of prairie, the soil is usually very moist most of the growing season, and has poor water drainage. This can possibly contain a bog or fen, since it often has plentiful stagnant water. This type of prairie has the best type of farming soil.

Mesic

Mesic prairies (English pronunciation: have good drainage, but have good soil during the growing season. This type of prairie is the most often converted for agricultural usage, consequently it is one of the more endangered types of prairie.

Dry

Dry Prairie is a prairie which has somewhat wet to very dry soil during the growing season because of good drainage in the soil. Often, this prairie can be found on uplands or slopes.

Farming

The very dense soil plagued the first settlers who were using wooden plows, which were more suitable for loose forest soil. On the prairie the plows bounced around and the soil stuck to them. This problem was solved in 1837 by an Illinois blacksmith named John Deere who developed a steel moldboard plow that was stronger and cut the roots, making the fertile soils ready for farming.

The tallgrass prairie has been converted into one of the most intensive crop producing areas in North America. Less than one tenth of one per cent (<0.09%) of the original landcover of the tallgrass prairie biome remains. States formerly with landcover in native tallgrass prairie such as Iowa, Illinois, Minnesota, Wisconsin, Nebraska, and Missouri have became valued for their highly productive soils and are included in the Corn Belt. As an example of this land use intensity, Illinois and Iowa for the United States, rank 49th and 50th out of 50 states in total uncultivated land remaining.

Biofuels

Researcher suggests that "biofuels made from high-diversity mixtures of prairie plants can reduce global warming by removing carbon dioxide from the atmosphere. Even when grown on infertile soils, they can provide a substantial portion of global energy needs, and leave fertile land for food production". Unlike corn and soybeans which are major food crops, prairie grasses are not used for human consumption. Prairie grasses can be grown in infertile soil, eliminating the cost of adding nutrients to the soil. Tilman and his colleagues estimate that prairie grass biofuels would yield 51 per cent more energy per acre than ethanol from corn grown on fertile land. Some grasses commonly used are lupine, big bluestem (turkey foot), blazing star, switchgrass, and prairie clover.

Preservation

Only one per cent of tallgrass prairie remains in the U.S. today.

Significant preserved areas of prairie include:

- American Prairie Foundation, Phillips and Blaine Counties, Montana
- Ceresco Prairie Conservancy, Ripon College, Wisconsin
- Clymer Meadow Preserve, Hunt County, Texas
- Cypress Hills Interprovincial Park, Alberta and Saskatchewan
- Grasslands National Park, Saskatchewan
- Hoosier Prairie, Lake County, Indiana
- Jennings Environmental Education Centre, Pennsylvania
- Kissimmee Prairie Preserve State Park, Okeechobee County, Florida
- Konza Prairie, Manhattan, Kansas
- Midewin National Tallgrass Prairie, in Will County, Illinois
- Neal Smith National Wildlife Refuge, Iowa

- Nine-Mile Prairie, Nebraska
- Paynes Prairie Preserve State Park, Alachua County, Florida
- Richard Bong State Recreation Area, in Kenosha County, Wisconsin
- Tallgrass Aspen Parkland, Manitoba & Minnesota
- Tallgrass Prairie National Preserve, Kansas
- Tallgrass Prairie Preserve 32,000 acres (130 km^2), Oklahoma
- University of Wisconsin–Madison Arboretum, University of Wisconsin–Madison, Wisconsin
- Zumwalt Prairie, Wallowa County, Oregon

Virgin Prairies

Virgin prairie refers to prairie land that has never been plowed. Small virgin prairies exist in the American Midwestern states and in Canada. Restored prairie refers to a prairie that has been reseeded after plowing or other disturbance.

Prairie Garden

A prairie garden is a garden primarily consisting of plants from a prairie.

Savanna

A savanna, or savannah, is a grassland ecosystem characterized by the trees being sufficiently small or widely spaced so that the canopy does not close. The open canopy allows sufficient light to reach the ground to support an unbroken herbaceous layer consisting primarily of C4 grasses. Some classification systems also recognize a grassland savanna from which trees are absent. This article deals only with savanna under the common definition of a grassy woodland with a significant woody plant component.

It is often believed that savannas feature widely spaced, scattered trees. However, in many savannas, tree densities are higher and trees are more regularly spaced than in forest. Savannas are also characterized by seasonal water availability, with the majority of rainfall confined to one season. Savannas are associated with several types of biomes. Savannas are frequently in a transitional zone between forest and desert or prairie. Savanna covers approximately 20 per cent of the Earth's land area. The largest area of savanna is in Africa.

Although the term *savanna* is believed to have originally come from an Arawak word describing 'land which is without trees but with much grass either tall or short' by the late 1800s it was used to mean 'land with both grass and trees'. It now refers to land with grass and either scattered trees or an open canopy of trees.

Spanish explorers familiar with the term 'sabana' called the grasslands they found around the Orinoco River 'llanos', as well as calling Venezuelan and Colombian grasslands by that specific term. 'Cerrado' was used on the higher savannas of the Brazilian Central Plateau.

Many grassy landscapes and mixed communities of trees, shrubs, and grasses were described as savanna before the middle of the 19th century, when the concept of a tropical savanna climate became established. The Köppen climate classification system was strongly influenced by effects of temperature and precipitation upon tree growth, and his over-simplified assumptions resulted in a tropical savanna classification concept which resulted in it being considered as a 'climatic climax' formation. The common usage meaning to describe vegetation now conflicts with a simplified yet widespread climatic concept meaning. The divergence has sometimes caused areas such as extensive savannas north and south of the Congo and Amazon Rivers to be excluded from mapped savanna categories.

'Barrens' has been used almost interchangeably with savanna in different parts of North America. Sometimes midwestern savanna were described as "grassland with trees". Different authors have defined the lower limits of savanna tree coverage as 5-10 per cent and upper limits range from 25-80 per cent of an area.

Two factors common to all savanna environments are rainfall variations from year to year, and dry season wildfires. Savannas around the world are also dominated by tropical grasses which use the C4 type of photosynthesis. In the Americas, e.g. in Belize, Central America, savanna vegetation is similar from Mexico to South America and to the Caribbean. In North America nearby trees are of subtropical types, ranging from southwestern Pinyon pine to southeastern Longleaf Pine and northern chestnut oak.

Savannas are subject to regular wildfires and the ecosystem appears to be the result of human use of fire. For example, Native Americans created the Pre-Columbian savannas of North America by periodically burning where fire-resistant plants were the dominant species. Pine barrens in scattered locations from New Jersey to coastal New England are remnants of these savannas. Aboriginal burning appears to have been responsible for the widespread occurrence of savanna in tropical Australia and New Guinea, and savannas in India are a result of human fire use. The maquis shrub savannas of the Mediterranean region were likewise created and maintained by anthropogenic fire.

These fires are usually confined to the herbaceous layer and do little long term damage to mature trees. However, these fires either kill or suppress tree seedlings, thus preventing the establishment of a continuous tree canopy which would prevent further grass growth. Prior to European settlement aboriginal land use practices, including fire, influenced vegetation and may have maintained and modified savanna flora. It has been suggested by many authors that aboriginal burning created a structurally more open savanna landscape. Aboriginal burning certainly created a habitat mosaic that probably increased biodiversity and changed the structure of woodlands and geographic range of numerous woodland species. t has been suggested by many authors that with the removal or alteration of traditional burning regimes many savannas are being replaced by forest and shrub thickets with little herbaceous layer.

The consumption of herbage by introduced grazers in savanna woodlands has led to a reduction in the amount of fuel available for burning and resulted in fewer and cooler fires. The introduction of exotic pasture legumes has also led to a reduction in the need to burn to produce a flush of green growth because legumes retain high nutrient levels throughout the year, and because fires can have a negative impact on legume populations which causes a reluctance to burn.

Grazing and Browsing Animals

The closed forests types such as broadleaf forests and rainforests are usually not grazed owing to the closed structure precluding grass growth, and hence offering little opportunity for grazing. In contrast the open structure of savannas allows the growth of a herbaceous layer and are commonly used for grazing domestic livestock. As a result much of the world's savannas have undergone change as a result of grazing by sheep, goats and cattle, ranging from changes in pasture composition to woody weed encroachment.

The removal of grass by grazing affects the woody plant component of woodland systems in two major ways. Grasses compete with woody plants for water in the topsoil and removal by grazing reduces this competitive effect, potentially boosting tree growth. In addition to this effect the removal of fuel reduces both the intensity and the frequency of fires which may control woody plant species. Grazing animals can have a more direct effect on woody plants by the browsing of palatable woody species. There is evidence that unpalatable woody plants have increased under grazing in savannas. Grazing also promotes the spread of weeds in savannas by the removal or reduction of the plants which would normally compete with potential weeds and hinder establishment. In addition to this, cattle and horses are implicated in the spread of the seeds of weed species such as Prickly Acacia (*Acacia nilotica*) and Stylo (*Stylosanthes* spp.). Alterations in savanna species composition brought about by grazing can alter ecosystem function, and are exacerbated by overgrazing and poor land management practices.

Introduced grazing animals can also affect soil condition through physical compaction and break-up of the soil caused by the hooves of animals and through the erosion effects caused by the removal of protective plant cover. Such effects are most likely to occur on land subjected to repeated and heavy grazing. The effects of overstocking are often worst on soils of low fertility and in low rainfall areas below 500 mm, as most soil nutrients in these areas tend to be concentrated in the surface so any movement of soils can lead to severe degradation. Alteration in soil structure and nutrient levels affects the establishment, growth and survival of plant species and in turn can lead to a change in woodland structure and composition.

Tree Clearing

Large areas of savanna have been cleared of trees, and this clearing is continuing today. For example until recently 480,000 ha of savanna were cleared annually in Australia alone primarily to improve pasture production. Substantial savanna areas have been cleared of woody vegetation and much of the area that remains today is vegetation that has been disturbed by either clearing or thinning at some point in the past.

Clearing is carried out by the grazing industry in an attempt to increase the quality and quantity of feed available for stock and to improve the management of livestock. The removal of trees from savanna land removes the competition for water from the grasses present, and can lead to a two to fourfold increase in pasture production, as well as improving the quality of the feed available. Since stock carrying capacity is strongly correlated with herbage yield there can be major financial benefits from the removal of trees. The removal of trees also assists grazing management. For example in sheep grazing regions of dense tree and shrub cover harbours predators, leading to increased stock losses while woody plant cover hinders mustering in both sheep and cattle areas.

A number of techniques have been employed to clear or kill woody plants in savannas. Early pastoralists used felling and girdling, the removal of a ring of bark and sapwood, as a means of clearing land. In the 1950s arboricides suitable for stem injection were developed. War-surplus heavy machinery was made available, and these were used for either pushing timber, or for pulling using a chain and ball strung between two machines. These two new methods of timber control, along with the introduction and widespread adoption of several new pasture grasses and legumes promoted a resurgence in tree clearing. The 1980s also saw the release of soil-applied arboricides, notably tebuthiuron, that could be utilised without cutting and injecting each individual tree.

In many ways 'artificial' clearing, particularly pulling, mimics the effects of fire and, in savannas adapted to regeneration after fire as most Queensland savannas are, there is a similar response to that after fire. Tree clearing in many savanna communities, although causing a dramatic reduction in basal area and canopy cover, often leaves a high percentage of woody plants alive either as seedlings too small to be affected or as plants capable of re-sprouting from lignotubers and broken stumps. A population of woody plants equal to half or more of the original number often remains following pulling of eucalypt communities, even if all the trees over 5 metres are uprooted completely.

Exotic Plant Species

A number of exotic plants species have been introduced to the savannas around the world. Amongst the woody plant species are serious environmental weeds such as Prickly Acacia (*Acacia nilotica*), Rubbervine (*Cryptostegia grandiflora*), Mesquite (*Prosopis* spp.), Lantana (*Lantana camara* and *L. montevidensis*) and Prickly Pear (*Opuntia* spp.) A range of herbaceous species have also been introduced to these woodlands, either deliberately or accidentally including Rhodes grass and other *Chloris* species, Buffel grass (*Cenchrus ciliaris*), Giant rat's tail grass (*Sporobolus pyramidalis*) parthenium (*Parthenium hysteropherus*) and stylos (*Stylosanthes* spp.) and other legumes. These introductions have the potential to significantly alter the structure and composition of savannas worldwide, and have already done so in many areas through a number of processes including altering the fire regime, increasing grazing pressure, competing with native vegetation and occupying previously vacant ecological niches. Other plant species include: white sage, spotted cactus, cotton seed, rosemary.

Climate Change

There exists the possibility that human induced climate change in the form of the greenhouse effect may result in an alteration of the structure and function of savannas. Some authors have suggested that savannas and grasslands may become even more susceptible to woody plant encroachment as a result of greenhouse induced climate change. However, a recent case described a savanna increasing its range at the expense of forest in response to climate variation, and potential exists for similar rapid, dramatic shifts in vegetation distribution as a result of global climate change, particularly at ecotones such as savannas so often represent.

Savanna Ecoregions

Savanna ecoregions are of several different types:

- **Tropical and subtropical savannas** are classified with tropical and subtropical grasslands and shrublands as the tropical and subtropical grasslands, savannas, and shrublands biome. The savannas of Africa, including the Serengeti, famous for its wildlife, are typical of this type.
- **Temperate savannas** are mid-latitude savannas with wetter summers and drier winters. They are classified with temperate savannas and shrublands as the temperate grasslands, savannas, and shrublands biome, that for example cover much of the Great Plains of the United States.
- **Mediterranean savannas** are mid-latitude savannas in Mediterranean climate regions, with mild, rainy winters and hot, dry summers, part of the Mediterranean forests,

woodlands, and scrub biome. The oak tree savannas of California, part of the California chaparral and woodlands ecoregion, fall into this category.

- **Flooded savannas** are savannas that are flooded seasonally or year-round. They are classified with flooded savannas as the flooded grasslands and savannas biome, which occurs mostly in the tropics and subtropics.
- **Montane** savannas are high-altitude savannas, located in a few spots around the world's high mountain regions, part of the montane grasslands and shrublands biome. The highland savannas of the Angolan Scarp savanna and woodlands ecoregion are an example.

Steppe

In physical geography, a steppe is an ecoregion, in the montane grasslands and shrublands and temperate grasslands, savannas, and shrublands biomes, characterized by grassland plains without trees apart from those near rivers and lakes. The prairie (especially the shortgrass and mixed prairie) is an example of a steppe, though it is not usually called such. It may be semi-desert, or covered with grass or shrubs or both, depending on the season and latitude. The term is also used to denote the climate encountered in regions too dry to support a forest, but not dry enough to be a desert. Soil type is typically chernozem.

Steppes are usually characterized by a semi-arid and continental climate. Extremes can be recorded in the summer of up to 40° C (104° F) and in winter, –40° C (–40° F). Besides this huge difference between summer and winter, the differences between day and night are also very great. In the highlands of Mongolia, 30° C (86° F) can be reached during the day with sub-zero °C (sub 32° F) readings at night.

The mid-latitude steppes can be summarised by hot summers and cold winters, averaging 250-500 mm (10-20 inches) of precipitation per year. Precipitation level alone is not what defines a steppe climate, potential evapotranspiration must also be taken into account.

Two types of steppe can be recorded:

1. *Temperate steppe:* The 'true' steppe, found in continental areas of the world; it can be further subdivided as seen here.
2. *Subtropical steppe:* A similar association of plants that can be found in the driest areas with a mediterranean-like climate; it has usually a short wet period

Peculiar types of steppe include shrub-steppe and alpine-steppe.

The world's largest steppe region, often referred to as 'the Great Steppe', is found in southwestern Russia and neighbouring countries in Central Asia, stretching from Ukraine in the west through Turkmenistan, Uzbekistan and Kazakhstan to the Altai, Koppet Dag and Tian Shan ranges.

The inner parts of Anatolia in Turkey, Central Anatolia and East Anatolia in particular and also some parts of Southeast Anatolia, as well as much of Armenia and Iran are largely dominated by cold steppe.

The Pannonian Plain is another steppe region in southeastern Europe, primarily Hungary.

Another large steppe area (prairie) is located in the central United States and western Canada. The shortgrass prairie steppe is the westernmost part of the Great Plains region. The Channeled Scablands in Southern British Columbia and Washington State are an example of a steppe region in North America outside of the Great Plains.

In South America, cold steppe can be found in Patagonia and much of the high elevation regions east of the southern Andes.

Relatively small steppe areas can be found in the interior of the South Island of New Zealand.

In Europe, some Mediterranean areas have a steppe-like vegetation, such as central Sicily, parts of Greece in the southern Athens area, and central-eastern Spain, especially the southeastern coast (around Murcia), and places cut off from adequate moisture due to rain shadow effects such as Zaragoza.

In Asia, a subtropical steppe can be found in semi-arid lands that fringe the Thar Desert of the Indian subcontinent.

In Australia, 'subtropical steppe' can found in a belt surrounding the most severe deserts of the continent and around the Musgrave Ranges. In North America this environment is typical of transition areas between zones with a Mediterranean climate and true deserts, such as Reno, Nevada, the inner part of California, and much of West Texas and adjacent areas in Mexico.

In South America the most important zone with a warm steppe is the Pampa.

Tropical Grasslands and Shrublands Similar to Steppe

Other zones dominated by grasslands and shrublands similar to steppe can be found in tropical areas of the world. In these locations, necessary rainfall to separate steppes from true deserts may be half as much again due to greater evapotranspiration. These include transition zones between savanna and severe desert such as the Sahel that fringes the true Sahara.

Another significant 'tropical steppe', noteworthy for not grading into desert, is the Sertão of northeastern Brazil.

Grasslands, mixture of grass, clover and other leguminous species, dicotyledonous, herbs and shrubs, contribute to a high degree to the struggle against erosion and to the regularizing of water regimes, to the purification of fertilizers and pesticides and to biodiversity and they have aesthetic role and recreational function as far as they provide public access that other agricultural uses do not allow. Grassland will continue to be an important form of land use in Europe, but with increased diversity in management objectives and systems used. Besides its role as basic nutrient for herbivores and ruminants, grasslands have opportunities for an adding value by exploiting positive health characteristics in animal products from grassland and through the delivery of environmental benefits. But even for grassland it is very difficult to create a good frame for its different tasks:

1. The provision of forage for livestock
2. Protection and conservation of soil and water resources
3. Furnishing a habitat for wildlife, both flora and fauna
4. Contribution to the attractiveness of the landscape.

Nevertheless it is the only crop able to fulfil so many tasks and to fit so many requirements. In this article the focus is limited to the grass and clover components of the grasslands.

Since mankind, human activities have been influencing grassland management. The most important one are the breeding activities since the early thirties in the last century. Improvement of yield and quality was not only in favour of agriculture, but also a lot of grass species were bred for amenity purposes, parks and sport fields.

Worldwide, grasslands cover about 3500 million ha, more than the double of arable land. On the European continent it is the opposite: only 230 million ha of grassland for 300 million ha of arable land, although, the 27 EU Member States converted about 4 million ha of grassland to arable land in the last twenty years, mostly to grow maize. Besides their natural aspect, grasslands have a pure agricultural destination as a primary food source for wild herbivores and domesticated ruminants. Actually, grasslands, being a mixture of different grass species, legumes and herbs, act as carbon sinks, erosion preventives, birds directive areas, habitat for small animals, nitrogen fixation source. As such, most grassland is in harmony and in balance with the environment, excepted intensively used ones.

No other crop in the world has such a wide range of applications and utilizations. In this paper we will summarise the importance of these different grassland functions:

1. The provision of forage for livestock
2. Protection and conservation of soil and water resources
3. Furnishing a habitat for wildlife, both flora and fauna
4. Contribution to the attractiveness of the landscape.

Although grasslands are a mixture of grass species, clover species and other leguminous, dicotyledonous, herbs and even shrubs, this paper focus only in detail to some characteristics of grass and clover species. Besides, there is only interest for improving yield and quality of a small number of grass and clover species.

Grass for Ruminants

In many countries of the world, pastoral rangelands are the primary and only resource on which both wild and domesticated herbivores depend. As the human population has increased, pastures has been converted into cropland, resulting in an overgrazing of the remaining grasslands.

The grassland area decreased in Western Europe with at least 8 million ha since the fifties. In the same period other traditional forage crops, like fodder beets and red clover almost disappeared, while the cultivation of the maize became more popular. Western European dairy farms are nowadays mostly based on the cultivation of two crops: grassland and maize.

Man's understanding of the principles of herbivore nutrition and the laboratory techniques to determine them, together with the plant yield and quality production have advanced significantly and nowadays, in intensive production systems, the dietary requirements are calculated with high precision.

Since World War II, plant breeding, land improvement and the use of fertilisers and pesticides have been applied as means of increasing primary production. In countries where pasture production is highly seasonal, countries with either cold winters or hot dry summers, feeding systems using cereals (especially maize cultivation) and protein-rich supplements (soybean meal), as well as crop by-products (sugar beet pulp, swill) have been developed to meet the nutritional needs of herbivores when there is insufficient grass to graze to meet the animals needs for maintenance, pregnancy and meat and milk production. In countries with plenty of cheap available cereals, pulses and crop by-products, feedlot systems have been developed in which cattle never feel a need to utilise pastoral resources at all. Since the bovine spongiform encephalopathy (BSE) crises an important protein rich by-product, meat and bone meal, is forbidden for incorporation and use in animal feed.

Grasslands and Food Supply

In the EU, there has been a continuous surplus of food products since 1980 and the common agricultural policy (CAP) has been reviewed and adapted several times. The last reform of 2003 intents:

- to contribute substantially to the stabilisation of the farmers' income and at the same time to the diversification of their farming activities;
- to be a credible answer to the demands of our citizens for healthy food, better quality, and environmentally sound production methods which respect animal welfare principles;
- to help to improve the public image of and support for the common agricultural policy; and
- to send a clear message to our trading partners, including in particular the developing countries.

In relation to plant products, animal products account for a relatively small proportion (< 10%) of food consumed by the human population of the world. However, if the people in the Third World attempt to obtain also 30 per cent of their calories from animal products, like we do, only a population of 2.5 billion people could be sustained. This is because of the low efficiency of conversion plant material into human food by livestock. Despite the relatively low contribution that herbivores make directly to the diet of the human population of the world, herbivores do have the ability to convert sources of protein and energy into food products that would otherwise be unavailable to humans. About a quarter of the total global land resource is represented by pastures suitable for utilisation by herbivores. From the 3500 million ha classified as grasslands, half of his area is indicated as natural grasslands. In the EU 15 we had in the year 2000 about 55 million ha of grasslands.

Since 1990 some 3 million hectares of grassland are converted to arable land, especially for maize cultivation. The EU enlarged its grassland area with about 20 million ha (+ 36%) and with 45 million ha of arable land (+ 53%), since the new membership of 12 CEEC countries.

Genetic Developments in Grasslands

The development of new varieties, better adapted to biotic and abiotic stress situations (diseases, climate) and the application of new technologies in pasture management with high fertiliser (nitrogen) input has resulted in a substantially increased output in yield and quality. Breeding work resulted in tetraploid varieties with some specific characteristics and interspecific crossing (cisgenese) grass species (e.g. *Festulolium* varieties). The possibilities of the characteristic pathways for C4 *Gramineae* for a more efficient water use, a higher dry matter production per unit of time and area and a higher N efficiency are only exploited in maize cultivation in temperate regions. Nevertheless productions of 10.000 litres of milk or 1000 kg of weight gain per ha of grassland are not exceptional. However, impacts of these technologies also cause problems of excessive manure, of air and water pollution and of perceptions with regard to the reductions in animal welfare. Problems with too high nitrate contents in water sources (> 50 mg/litre), too excessive N, P and K balances on dairy farms and unnatural veterinarian help with 'caesarean section' for high muscled cows at calving, drove dairy farming far away from the original sustainable production system. Moreover, the disappearance of the complex grass-clover-herbs mixtures by converting native grasslands into monocultures of perennial ryegrass results in a deterioration of the biodiversity. Some specific forage crops like red clover, alfalfa, vetches, fodder beets, etc. disappeared on the much specialised dairy farms. Intensively managed grassland for grazing (summer time) and maize for silage (winter feeding) are almost the two only pillars of the modern dairy farming system in the EU. These negative impacts are no longer politically acceptable and statutory regulations (specific EU regulations and directives) are progressively being introduced to control them.

In July 2002 the European Commission recommended guidelines (2003/556/EC) for the development of national strategies and best practices to ensure the coexistence of genetically modified crops with conventional and organic farming. Up to now there seems to be no interest in changing grasses by genetic engineering, may be because of the difficulties with the interspecific crossing possibilities and the permanent character of grass species (the more permanent and persistent the variety, the less renovation is needed).

Grassland Composition

Two types of grass species dominate grasslands at the global scale: C3 and C4 species; depending on the first carbohydrate synthesised during the photosynthesis. In Europe most of the grass species belong to the C3 group. Their optimal temperature for photosynthesis, on average 20°C, is much lower than for C4 grass species (on average 30°C) and they still have photosynthetic activity above 5°C. Therefore C3 grass species are much more adapted to grow and to develop in the colder regions. The most important grass species in natural and renovated grassland in Europe is perennial ryegrass (*Lolium perenne* L.). Other important grass species, especially because of their production and/or quality characteristics are Italian ryegrass (*Lolium multiflorum* Lam.), tall fescue (*Festuca arundinacea* L.), meadow fescue (*Festuca pratensis* Hudson), cocksfoot (*Dactylis glomerata* L.), timothy (*Phleum pratense* L.), rough-stalked meadowgrass (*Poa trivialis* L.), smooth-stalked meadowgrass (*Poa pratensis* L.) and bent (*Agrostis spp*).

Besides dicotyledonous plant species (*Taraxacum officinale, Capsela bursa pastoris*), white clover is normally a big part of the botanical composition, especially in natural grasslands and in renovated grassland depending to the sown grass-clover mixture the grassland management (nitrogen fertilisation, cutting regime, grazing density) and season (white clover develops best in summer, while grass species grow better in springtime). The interest for white clover in grassland is renewed since the last decades for its nitrogen symbiosis capacity, due to the limited nitrogen fertilisation of grassland in EU member states, because of the problems caused by nitrate in the soil. A good and stable balance between grasses, clover and dicotyledonous species is difficult to reach and to maintain during the whole grazing season. A lot of research data and an enormous quantity of literature about the role of white clover in grassland are available.

In old permanent pastures in Europe, America and Canada one can find grasses infected with endophytes. The most common endpophyte is *(Acremonium) Neotyphodium coenophialum* L. in ryegrass and festuca grass species. Grasses infected with this endophyte produce more alkaloids, like perloline, loline and lolitrem and show a better resistance against stress (drought and diseases). Publications from American, Canadian and New Zealander authors prove negative animal behaviours (higher temperature, fescued foot, ergotisme) of cattle grazing infected grass, while European researchers never concluded to such negative effects.

The last couple of years there is a lot of interest for the nutritive role of grassland in producing conjugated linoleic acid (CLA) and fatty acids. Grasses contain linoleic acid and over half of the total fatty acids consist of .-3 linoleic acid C 18 : 3n-3). Substantial bio hydrogenation occurs in the rumen, but some of this linoleic acid is absorbed from the digestive tract and appears in ruminant products. Studies by researcher show substantial differences in contents of .-3 linoleic acids between grass species and cultivars. There is obvious potential to exploit this finding in marketing products from grass-based cattle breeding. More research is needed to establish the factors determining the extent of bio hydrogenation of these fatty acids in the rumen and to develop methods for minimising these changes. Conjugated linoleic acid (CLA) is a potent anti-carcinogen. Linoleic acid has 2 unsaturated positions: position 9 and 11. This unusual structure is associated with remarkable characteristics: the fat and protein metabolism of the body is regulated by an increased muscle formation and a decreased fat content. Milk and meat produced by grazing cattle contain this CLA and have in this respect a much higher nutritive value for mankind.

Grass on Dikes, Verges and Nature Reserves

Grasses are the main plant species in verges along roads, railways and on river dikes. It is difficult to get an idea how many hectares are involved in this type of land cover. Along highways, main and small roads, along railways and rivers, strips of some metres of width all over hundreds of kilometres are overgrown with grass, herbs, shrubs and trees. One may count some 3000 m^2 of verges per running km, giving an enormous capacity for carbon sequestration, mostly for a long period of time. Besides the presence of grass species in fallow terrains are also an enormous carbon sink, although in these sites the situation lasts for a long period so that C balance does not change.

In the frame of the EU Directive 2078/92 “Farming practices compatible with the requirements of protection of the environment and natural resources, as well as maintenance of the countryside and the landscape”, the member states may conclude agreements with farmers for sowing grass or another cover crop after a main crop (cereals, maize) to prevent the leaching of nitrates and minerals and to prevent wind and water erosion during winter time. In Flanders, the Government contracted 4.240 farmers with about 50.000 hectares for this arrangement in 2006. Under the same Directive, the authorities can make a long term agreement (5-10 years) with farmers for the management of buffer zones (5 m width) between arable land along small streams or a wood for an increasing biodiversity. In Flanders, it means a total area of 1.600 ha under this management system.

In more modern times (1950s) the sugar industry used vetiver grass quite widely as contour conservation hedges and for the stabilization of road sides and embankments. Vetiver once thought to be confined to wetlands thrives over a range of ecological conditions.

In cases, set-aside and riparian buffer zones and woods, concern arable land converted to grassland. But this is only a small fraction of the grassland area lost in Europe during the last decades.

It is clear that these types of grasslands respond very much to the new EU policy for maintaining and enlarging the biodiversity, animal welfare, development of the countryside, etc., directed in the respective regulations and directives.

Grass for Amenity Purposes

There are a lot of small, varying to very large, grass fields without any agricultural function. More and more agricultural land is used for the urbanisation and the construction of public buildings and private houses. Part of it is reserved for parks and lawns. The private garden and especially the 'green grass of home' is in many countries for families the identification of their good feelings. People try to keep their lawn in good condition and even to make it better looking. For private and public organisations parks, sport fields and open areas are mainly composed of different grasses. Mostly specific grass species are bred for these purposes, giving a strong dense green sward, composed of slow growing grasses with good carrying capacity. These grass fields are frequently renovated and the most appropriate species and varieties are used to fit with the requested goal. Besides its amenity role, this type of grassland has almost no other side functions; just its water holding capacity and erosion protection effect are positive factors. For carbon sequestration, development of the biodiversity and improvement of fauna and flora, amenity grass fields seem not be very useful.

In well developed countries, the production of ornamental plants (azaleas roses) is big business, while in other parts of the world drug crops (tobacco, cannabis) are grown. To survive, in Africa and other poor countries, the production of food and feed is the most important. A discussion about the possibility to produce the five Fs (food, feed, fibre, fuel and/or fun) is only speculative in rich and well developed areas.

Grass As Energy and Fuel Crop

At the end of 2010 the minimum proportion of bio fuels or other renewable fuels on the market of EU member states must be 5.75 per cent by Directive 2003/30/EC. Research and industry are looking for crop production systems that give biomass productions transferable to bio energy: bio fuels from cell walls.

Poplar, willow, perennial grass species *Miscanthus* and wheat straw, recognized as energy crop for the second generation fuel, are the main sources of biomass relevant to the member states of EU. The currently available biomass for non-food use could be increased by proper selection of the plant species taking in consideration the specificities of particular region. The development of breeding programmes for the energy crops based on the scientific findings of plant system biology will allow economically more efficient plants to be selected. Plant genetic modification of these plants via gene transfer methods, is an option for the development of new forms possessing valuable traits such as resistance to biotic and abiotic stress, lower inputs of fertilizers and higher yield of biomass. Obviously this approach has a future, but presently as a whole, the public opinion especially in some countries of the European Union is not positive towards the GMO's.

Poplar tress are transformed in Plant Genetic Systems (Ghent University, Belgium) with a much better cell wall digestibility (lower lignin content); but the Belgian policy didn't allow to grow them outside up to now. Nevertheless the genetically modified crops for energy purposes will be more easily accepted from all stakeholders than transgenic food crops.

Grass for Carbon Sequestration and for Charcoal

Other specific characteristics give grassland more importance. The capacity to store carbon and to act as a carbon sink, in comparison to arable land, its role in the prevention of erosion, the immobilisation of leaching minerals are interesting additional effects in the frame of a sustainable agriculture and development of the countryside.

Grasslands are able to sequester about the double quantity of C in the soil in comparison to arable land.

In this context is worthwhile to notice that permanent grasslands are sinks for carbon sequestration in comparison to arable land. Although livestock enteric fermentation, manure and the use of inorganic fertilizer account for the major share of agricultural greenhouse gasses (GHG) in most developed countries. In the EU, the contribution of agriculture in the total main GHG, carbon dioxide CO_2 is only about 2 per cent, it accounts for over 50 per cent of total nitrous oxide N_2O and nearly 45 per cent of methane CH_4 emissions. Besides, the global warming potential of CH_4 and N_2O are respectively about 20 and 300 times higher than that of CO_2. So some agricultural activities, especially well fertilised grazed grassland and grassland renovation by ploughing the old sward may lead to high GHG emissions and transform grassland from a carbon sink to a carbon source.

In some countries, especially in C&E European countries (Romania, Bulgaria), farmers have the tradition to burn the stubbles after the harvest. Under this uncontrolled burning, black parts of stems remain. Under controlled anaerobe combustion of plants (300 to 600°C, depending of the technology), volatile components (oils) are collected. The remaining ash is called charcoal. This can be used to improve soil characteristics. Depending of composition of the mixture of grass species, herbs and shrubs, the nature of volatile components will change and so also the composition and characteristics of the charcoal.

Grass for Perfumes, Alcohols and Beverages

Well known is the kind of brandy 'Zubrowka bison grass wodka' from Poland with a stem of bison grass (sweet grass: *Hierochloe odorata* L.) as a characteristic in the bottle.

Other coumarin rich grass species are used in the same way, like sweet vernal grass (*Anthoxanthum odoratum* L.) used in tobacco and herb pillows.

There are twelve known varieties of vetiver grass; the most important is *Vetiveria zizanioides* Linn. For centuries the oil extract from the roots of *V. zizanioides* has been used in the perfume trade. Indigenous peoples have recognized vetiver for its medicinal uses, for thatching, mulch, and feed, and for soil and moisture conservation. It grows both on highly acidic (< pH 4) and alkaline soils (pH 11). Its roots will grow to depths of 3-4 metres. It is not affected seriously by pests or diseases. Each clump of vetiver is extremely dense, so dense that if con*Fig*.d correctly will act as a near perfect filter. The generic name Vetiver is a Tamil word meaning 'root that is dug up' and zizanioides means 'by the riverside'.

The genus *Cymbopogon* accumulates different kinds of essential oils. The essential oil of *Cymbopogon validus*, which chemical composition is reported by Chagonda *et al.* (2000), has been used as an astringent skin toner and anti-ageing for men and has anti fungal and anti septic properties. The predominant compounds, properties and uses of *Cymbopogon* species are described by researcher.

The essential oil of lemon grass *Cymbopogon citratus* (West Indian lemon grass) consists mainly of citral. Further terpenoids in lemon grass oil are nerol, limonene, linalool and ß-caryophyllene. The content of myrcene is low, but still enough to make the oil susceptible to oxidative polymerization.

East Indian lemon grass *Cymbopogon flexuosus* oil consists of alcohols citronellol, geraniol) and aldehydes (geranial, neral, citronellal). This species is dominantly used in the perfume industry as it contains less myrcene and, therefore, has a longer shelf life.

Two further species have considerable relevance for the perfume industry: The so-called palmarosa oil is distilled from *Cymbopogon martini* (Roxb.) J.F. Watson var. mar tini (native to India, cultivated also in Jawa) and contains mainly geraniol and geranyl acetate. Also worth mentioning is citronella grass (*Cymbopogon winterianus* Jowitt) which also stems from India, but is today grown throughout the tropics; its main constituents are citronellal, geraniol and citronellol plus minor amounts of geranyl acetate.

EU Policy and Grasslands

The EU policy has always stimulated intensive farming without encouraging employment. For some cops yield per ha doubled since 1960, but in the meantime the number of farmers has decreased drastically to about 2 per cent of the active population. It is difficult to understand the logic that the former CAP favoured the production of one ha of silage corn to one hectare of grassland ten times more aid. The challenges we had in the West to face at the end of World War II, being cut from our traditional wheat sources, located at the other side of the 'Iron Curtain' are disappeared. Between 2004 and 2007, 12 new countries got the EU membership. Most of these countries have a less intensively developed agriculture than the EU 15 with on average about 15 per cent of their people, being active in agriculture. Hopefully the newest CAP vision of the EU, promoting and supporting a less intensive agriculture with a multifunctional task for the farmer will fit with the development of these CEEC countries so that within a decade all members of the CEEC will aim the same goal: a good balance between the social, environmental and economic aspects of agriculture.

The renewed and actualised CAP of the EU (Council Regulation EC No 1782/2003, implemented by the Commission Regulation (EC) No 1973/2004) makes grasslands nowadays more attractive for farmers than before. Article 5.2 of this Council Regulation obligates Member States to ensure all that land which was under permanent pasture at the date provided for the area aid applications for 2003 to be mentioned under permanent pasture. In annex IV the standards for 'Good agricultural and environmental conditions' (GAEC) are mentioned with special attention for permanent pasture. The Member States themselves must introduce their own policy in the development of these GAEC, so that the farmers will receive direct payments in return for their responsibilities towards the protection of the environment, animal health and welfare and public health (so called 'Cross Compliance').

Grassland will continue to be an important form of land use in Europe, but with increased diversity in management objectives and systems used. There are opportunities for adding value by exploiting positive health characteristics in animal products from grassland and through the delivery of environmental benefits. In fact grasslands contribute to a high degree to the struggle against erosion and to the regularisation of water regimes, to the purification of fertilizers and pesticides and to biodiversity. Finally they have an aesthetic role and recreational function as far as they provide public access that other agricultural uses do not allow.

The evolution of policies that seek to enhance the environmental performance of agriculture will present major challenge to farmers, the agro-food industry, trade relations and policy makers. This will involve reconciling the trade-offs between the need to increase agricultural production to provide food and other agricultural products and services at affordable prices, addressing the social concerns of rural communities, while enhancing environmental conditions in agriculture and expanding trade. The European agricultural policy is not simple and needs to accommodate also social and environmental requirements. Even for grassland it is very difficult to create a good frame for its different tasks:

1. The provision of forage for livestock
2. Protection and conservation of soil and water resources
3. Furnishing a habitat for wildlife, both flora and fauna
4. Contribution to the attractiveness of the landscape.

Nevertheless, it is the only crop able to fulfil so many tasks and to fit so many requirements.

13

Evolution Mechanism in Forest Plants

The Evolution of Plants

The evolution of plants has resulted in increasing levels of complexity, from the earliest algal mats, through bryophytes, lycopods, ferns to the complex gymnosperms and angiosperms of today. While the groups which appeared earlier continue to thrive, especially in the environments in which they evolved, each new grade of organisation has eventually become more 'successful' than its predecessors by most measures.

Probably an algal scum formed on land 1,200 million years ago. In the Ordovician period, around 450 million years ago, the first land plants appeared. These began to diversify in the late Silurian Period, around 420 million years ago, and the fruits of their diversification are displayed in remarkable detail in an early Devonian fossil assemblage from the Rhynie chert. This chert preserved early plants in cellular detail, petrified in volcanic springs. By the middle of the Devonian Period most of the features recognised in plants today are present, including roots, leaves and secondary wood, and by late Devonian times seeds had evolved. Late Devonian plants had thereby reached a degree of sophistication that allowed them to form forests of tall trees. Evolutionary innovation continued after the Devonian period. Most plant groups were relatively unscathed by the Permo-Triassic extinction event, although the structures of communities changed. This may have set the scene for the evolution of flowering plants in the Triassic (~200 million years ago), which exploded in the Cretaceous and Tertiary. The latest major group of plants to evolve were the grasses, which became important in the mid Tertiary, from around 40 million years ago. The grasses, as well as many other groups, evolved new mechanisms of metabolism to survive the low CO_2 and warm, dry conditions of the tropics over the last 10 million years.

Land plants evolved from chlorophyte algae, perhaps as early as 510 million years ago; their closest living relatives are the charophytes, specifically Charales. Assuming that the Charales' habit has changed little since the divergence of lineages, this means that the land plants evolved from a branched, filamentous, haplontic alga, dwelling in shallow fresh water, perhaps at the edge of seasonally desiccating pools. Co-operative interactions with fungi may have helped early plants adapt to the stresses of the terrestrial realm.

Plants were not the first photosynthesisers on land, though: consideration of weathering rates suggests that organisms were already living on the land 1,200 million years ago, and microbial fossils have been found in freshwater lake deposits from 1,000 million years ago, but the carbon isotope record suggests that they were too scarce to impact the atmospheric composition until around 850 million years were probably small and simple, forming little more than an 'algal scum'.

The first evidence of plants on land comes from spores of Mid-Ordovician age (early Llanvirn, ~470 million years ago). These spores, known as cryptospores, were produced either singly (monads), in pairs (diads) or groups of four (tetrads), and their microstructure resembles that of modern liverwort spores, suggesting they share an equivalent grade of organisation. They are composed of sporopollenin – further evidence of an embryophytic affinity. It could be that atmospheric 'poisoning' prevented eukaryotes from colonising the land prior to this, or it could simply have taken a great time for the necessary complexity to evolve.

Trilete spores similar to those of vascular plants appear soon afterwards, in Upper Ordovician rocks. Depending exactly when the tetrad splits, each of the four spores may bear a 'trilete mark', a *Y*-shape, reflecting the points at which each cell squashed up against its neighbours. However, this requires that the spore walls be sturdy and resistant at an early stage. This resistance is closely associated with having a desiccation-resistant outer wall—a trait only of use when spores must survive out of water. Indeed, even those embryophytes that have returned to the water lack a resistant wall, thus don't bear trilete marks. A close examination of algal spores shows that none have trilete spores, either because their walls are not resistant enough, or in those rare cases where it is, the spores disperse before they are squashed enough to develop the mark, or don't fit into a tetrahedral tetrad.

The earliest megafossils of land plants were thalloid organisms, which dwelt in fluvial wetlands and are found to have covered most of an early Silurian flood plain. They could only survive when the land was waterlogged. There were also microbial mats.

Once plants had reached the land, there were two approaches to dealing with desiccation. The bryophytes avoid it or give in to it, restricting their ranges to moist settings, or drying out and putting their metabolism 'on hold' until more water arrives. Tracheophytes resist desiccation. They all bear a waterproof outer cuticle layer wherever they are exposed to air (as do some bryophytes), to reduce water loss, but—since a total covering would cut them off from CO_2 in the atmosphere—they rapidly evolved stomata, small openings to allow gas exchange. Tracheophytes also developed vascular tissue to aid in the movement of water within the organisms, and moved away from a gametophyte dominated life cycle. Vascular tissue also facilitated upright growth without the support of water and paved the way for the evolution of larger plants on land.

The establishment of a land-based flora caused increased accumulation of oxygen in the atmosphere, as the plants produced oxygen as a waste product. When this concentration rose above 13 per cent, wildfires became possible. This is first recorded in the early Silurian fossil record by charcoalified plant fossils. Apart from a controversial gap in the Late Devonian, charcoal is present ever since.

Charcoalification is an important taphonomic mode. Wildfire drives off the volatile compounds, leaving only a shell of pure carbon. This is not a viable food source for herbivores or detritovores, so is prone to preservation; it is also robust, so can withstand pressure and display exquisite, sometimes sub-cellular, detail.

All multicellular plants have a life cycle comprising two generations or phases. One is termed the gametophyte, has a single set of chromosomes (denoted 1N), and produces gametes (sperm and eggs). The other is termed the sporophyte, has paired chromosomes (denoted 2N), and produces spores. The gametophyte and sporophyte may appear identical – homomorphy – or may be very different – heteromorphy.

The pattern in plant evolution has been a shift from homomorphy to heteromorphy. The algal ancestors to land plants were almost certainly haplobiontic, being haploid for all their life cycles, with a unicellular zygote providing the 2N stage. All land plants (i.e. embryophytes) are diplobiontic – that is, both the haploid and diploid stages are multicellular. Two trends are apparent: bryophytes (liverworts, mosses and hornworts) have developed the gametophyte, with the sporophyte becoming almost entirely dependent on it; vascular plants have developed the sporophyte, with the gametophyte being particularly reduced in the seed plants.

The interpolation theory (also known as the antithetic or intercalary theory) holds that the sporophyte phase was a fundamentally new invention, caused by the mitotic division of a freshly germinated zygote, continuing until meiosis produces spores. This theory implies that the first sporophytes bore a very different morphology that the gametophyte they depended on. This seems to fit well with what we know of the bryophytes, in which a vegetative thalloid gametophyte is parasitised by simple sporophytes, which often comprise no more than a sporangium on a stalk. Increasing complexity of the ancestrally simple sporophyte, including the eventual acquisition of photosynthetic cells, would free it from its dependence on a gametophyte, as we see in some hornworts (*Anthoceros*), and eventually result in the sporophyte developing organs and vascular tissue, and becoming the dominant phase, as in the tracheophytes (vascular plants). This theory may be supported by observations that smaller *Cooksonia* individuals must have been supported by a gametophyte generation. The observed appearance of larger axial sizes, with room for photosynthetic tissue and thus self-sustainability, provides a possible route for the development of a self-sufficient sporophyte phase.

The alternative hypothesis is termed the transformation theory (or homologous theory). This posits that the sporophyte appeared suddenly by a delay in the occurrence of meiosis after the zygote germinated. Since the same genetic material would be employed, the haploid and diploid phases would look the same. This explains the behaviour of some algae, which produce alternating phases of identical sporophytes and gametophytes. Subsequent adaption to the desiccating land environment, which makes sexual reproduction difficult, would result in the simplification of the sexually active gametophyte, and elaboration of the sporophyte phase to better disperse the waterproof spores. The tissue of sporophytes and gametophytes preserved in the Rhynie chert is of similar complexity, which is taken to support this hypothesis.

To photosynthesise, plants must absorb CO_2 from the atmosphere. However, this comes at a price: while stomata are open to allow CO_2 to enter, water can evaporate. Water is lost much faster than CO_2 is absorbed, so plants need to replace it, and have developed systems to transport water from the moist soil to the site of photosynthesis. Early plants sucked water between the walls of their cells, then evolved the ability to control water loss (and CO_2 acquisition) through the use of stomata. Specialised water transport tissues soon evolved in the form of hydroids, tracheids, then secondary xylem, followed by an endodermis and ultimately vessels.

The high CO_2 levels of Silurian-Devonian times, when plants were first colonising land, meant that the need for water was relatively low . As CO_2 was withdrawn from the atmosphere by plants, more water was lost in its capture, and more elegant transport mechanisms evolved. As water transport mechanisms, and waterproof cuticles, evolved, plants could survive without being continually covered by a film of water. This transition from poikilohydry to homoiohydry opened up new potential for colonisation. Plants then needed a robust internal structure that held long narrow channels for transporting water from the soil to all the different parts of the above-soil plant, especially to the parts where photosynthesis occurred.

During the Silurian, CO_2 was readily available, so little water needed expending to acquire it. By the end of the Carboniferous, when CO_2 levels had lowered to something approaching today's, around 17 times more water was lost per unit of CO_2 uptake. However, even in these "easy" early days, water was at a premium, and had to be transported to parts of the plant from the wet soil to avoid desiccation. This early water transport took advantage of the cohesion-tension mechanism inherent in water. Water has a tendency to diffuse to areas that are drier, and this process is accelerated when water can be wicked along a fabric with small spaces. In small passages, such as that between the plant cell walls (or in tracheids), a column of water behaves like rubber – when molecules evaporate from one end, they literally pull the molecules behind them along the channels. Therefore transpiration alone provided the driving force for water transport in early plants. However, without dedicated transport vessels, the cohesion-tension mechanism cannot transport water more than about 2 cm, severely limiting the size of the earliest plants. This process demands a steady supply of water from one end, to maintain the chains; to avoid exhausing it, plants developed a waterproof cuticle. Early cuticle may not have had pores but did not cover the entire plant surface, so that gas exchange could continue. However, dehydration at times was inevitable; early plants cope with this by having a lot of water stored between their cell walls, and when it comes to it sticking out the tough times by putting life 'on hold' until more water is supplied.

To be free from the constraints of small size and constant moisture that the parenchymatic transport system inflicted, plants needed a more efficient water transport system. During the early Silurian, they developed specialized cells, which were lignified (or bore similar chemical compounds) to avoid implosion; this process coincided with cell death, allowing their innards to be emptied and water to be passed through them. These wider, dead, empty cells were a million times more conductive than the inter-cell method, giving the potential for transport over longer distances, and higher CO_2 diffusion rates.

The first macrofossils to bear water-transport tubes *in situ* are the early Devonian pretracheophytes *Aglaophyton* and *Horneophyton*, which have structures very similar to the hydroids of modern mosses. Plants continued to innovate new ways of reducing the resistance to flow within their cells, thereby increasing the efficiency of their water transport. Bands on the walls of tubes, in fact apparent from the early Silurian onwards, are an early improvisation to aid the easy flow of water. Banded tubes, as well as tubes with pitted ornamentation on their walls, were lignified and, when they form single celled conduits, are considered to be tracheids. These, the 'next generation' of transport cell design, have a more rigid structure than hydroids, allowing them to cope with higher levels of water pressure. Tracheids may have a single evolutionary origin, possibly within the hornworts, uniting all tracheophytes.

Water transport requires regulation, and dynamic control is provided by stomata. By adjusting the amount of gas exchange, they can restrict the amount of water lost through transpiration. This is an important role where water supply is not constant, and indeed stomata appear to have evolved before tracheids, being present in the non-vascular hornworts.

An endodermis probably evolved during the Silu-Devonian, but the first fossil evidence for such a structure is Carboniferous. This structure in the roots covers the water transport tissue and regulates ion exchange (and prevents unwanted pathogens etc. from entering the water transport system). The endodermis can also provide an upwards pressure, forcing water out of the roots when transpiration is not enough of a driver.

Once plants had evolved this level of controlled water transport, they were truly homoiohydric, able to extract water from their environment through root-like organs rather than relying on a film of surface moisture, enabling them to grow to much greater size. As a result of their independence from their surroundings, they lost their ability to survive desiccation – a costly trait to retain.

During the Devonian, maximum xylem diametre increased with time, with the minimum diametre remaining pretty constant. By the middle Devonian, the tracheid diametre of some plant lineages had plateaued. Wider tracheids allow water to be transported faster, but the overall transport rate depends also on the overall cross-sectional area of the xylem bundle itself. The increase in vascular bundle thickness further seems to correlate with the width of plant axes, and plant height; it is also closely related to the appearance of leaves and increased stomatal density, both of which would increase the demand for water.

While wider tracheids with robust walls make it possible to achieve higher water transport pressures, this increases the problem of cavitation. Cavitation occurs when a bubble of air forms within a vessel, breaking the bonds between chains of water molecules and preventing them from pulling more water up with their cohesive tension. A tracheid, once cavitated, cannot have its embolism removed and return to service (except in a few advanced angiosperms which have developed a mechanism of doing so). Therefore it is well worth plants' while to avoid cavitation occurring. For this reason, pits in tracheid walls have very small diametres, to prevent air entering and allowing bubbles to nucleate. Freeze-thaw cycles are a major cause of cavitation. Damage to a tracheid's wall almost inevitably leads to air leaking in and cavitation, hence the importance of many tracheids working in parallel.

Cavitation is hard to avoid, but once it has occurred plants have a range of mechanisms to contain the damage. Small pits link adjacent conduits to allow fluid to flow between them, but not air – although ironically these pits, which prevent the spread of embolisms, are also a major cause of them. These pitted surfaces further reduce the flow of water through the xylem by as much as 30 per cent. Conifers, by the Jurassic, developed an ingenious improvement, using valve-like structures to isolate cavitated elements. These torus-margo structures have a blob floating in the middle of a donut; when one side depressurises the blob is sucked into the torus and blocks further flow. Other plants simply accept cavitation; for instance, oaks grow a ring of wide vessels at the start of each spring, none of which survive the winter frosts. Maples use root pressure each spring to force sap upwards from the roots, squeezing out any air bubbles.

Growing to height also employed another trait of tracheids – the support offered by their lignified walls. Defunct tracheids were retained to form a strong, woody stem, produced in most instances by a secondary xylem. However, in early plants, tracheids were too mechanically vulnerable, and retained a central position, with a layer of tough sclerenchyma on the outer rim of the stems. Even when tracheids do take a structural role, they are supported by sclerenchymatic tissue.

Tracheids end with walls, which impose a great deal of resistance on flow; vessel members have perforated end walls, and are arranged in series to operate as if they were one continuous vessel. The function of end walls, which were the default state in the Devonian, was probably to avoid embolisms. An embolism is where an air bubble is created in a tracheid. This may happen as a result of freezing, or by gases dissolving out of solution. Once an embolism is formed, it usually cannot be removed (but see later); the affected cell cannot pull water up, and is rendered useless.

The size of tracheids is limited as they comprise a single cell; this limits their length, which in turn limits their maximum useful diametre to 80 μm. Conductivity grows with the fourth power of diametre, so increased diametre has huge rewards; vessel elements, consisting of a number of cells, joined at their ends, overcame this limit and allowed larger tubes to form, reaching diametres of up to 500 μm, and lengths of up to 10 m.

Vessels first evolved during the dry, low CO_2 periods of the late Permian, in the horsetails, ferns and Selaginellales independently, and later appeared in the mid Cretaceous in angiosperms and gnetophytes. Vessels allow the same cross-sectional area of wood to transport around a hundred times more water than tracheids! This allowed plants to fill more of their stems with structural fibres, and also opened a new niche to vines, which could transport water without being as thick as the tree they grew on. Despite these advantages, tracheid-based wood is a lot lighter, thus cheaper to make, as vessels need to be much more reinforced to avoid cavitation.

Leaves today are, in almost all instances, an adaptation to increase the amount of sunlight that can be captured for photosynthesis. Leaves certainly evolved more than once, and probably originated as spiny outgrowths to protect early plants from herbivory.

Leaves are the Primary Photosynthetic Organs of a Plant

Leaves are the primary photosynthetic organs of a plant. Based on their structure, they are classified into two types - microphylls, that lack complex venation patterns and megaphylls, that are large and with a complex venation. It has been proposed that these structures arose independently. Megaphylls, according to the Telome hypothesis, have evolved from plants that showed a three dimensional branching architecture, through three transformations—planation, which involved formation of a planar architecture, webbing, or formation of the outgrowths between the planar branches and fusion, where these webbed outgrowths fused to form a proper leaf lamina. All three steps happened multiple times in the evolution of today's leaves.

It has been proposed that the before the evolution of leaves, plants had the photosynthetic apparatus on the stems. Today's megaphyll leaves probably became commonplace some 360mya, about 40my after the simple leafless plants had colonized the land in the early Devonian period. This spread has been linked to the fall in the atmospheric carbon dioxide concentrations in the Late Paleozoic era associated with a rise in density of stomata on leaf surface. This must have allowed for better transpiration rates and gas exchange. Large leaves with less stomata would have gotten heated up in the sun's heat, but an increased stomatal density allowed for a better-cooled leaf, thus making its spread feasible.

The rhyniophytes of the Rhynie chert comprised nothing more than slender, unornamented axes. The early to middle Devonian trimerophytes, therefore, are the first evidence we have of anything that could be considered leafy. This group of vascular plants are recognisable by their masses of terminal sporangia, which adorn the ends of axes which may bifurcate or trifurcate. Some organisms, such as *Psilophyton*, bore enations. These are small, spiny outgrowths of the stem, lacking their own vascular supply.

Around the same time, the zosterophyllophytes were becoming important. This group is recognisable by their kidney-shaped sporangia, which grew on short lateral branches close to the main axes. They sometimes branched in a distinctive H-shape. The majority of this group bore pronounced spines on their axes. However, none of these had a vascular trace, and the first evidence of vascularised enations occurs in the Rhynie genus *Asteroxylon*. The spines of *Asteroxylon* had a primitive vasuclar supply – at the very least, leaf traces could be seen departing from the central protostele towards each individual 'leaf'. A fossil known as *Baragwanathia* appears in the fossil record slightly earlier, in the late Silurian. In this organism, these leaf traces continue into the leaf to form their mid-vein. One theory, the 'enation theory', holds that the leaves developed by outgrowths of the protostele connecting with existing enations, but it is also possible that microphylls evolved by a branching axis forming 'webbing'.

Asteroxylon and *Baragwanathia* are widely regarded as primitive lycopods. The lycopods are still extant today, familiar as the quillwort *Isoetes* and the club mosses. Lycopods bear distinctive microphylls – leaves with a single vascular trace. Microphylls could grow to some size – the Lepidodendrales boasted microphylls over a metre in length – but almost all just bear the one vascular bundle. (An exception is the branching *Selaginella*).

The more familiar leaves, megaphylls, are thought to have separate origins – indeed, they appeared four times independently, in the ferns, horsetails, progymnosperms, and seed plants. They appear to have originated from dichotomising branches, which first overlapped (or 'overtopped') one another, and eventually developed 'webbing' and evolved into gradually more leaf-like structures. So megaphylls, by this 'teleome theory', are composed of a group of webbed branches – hence the 'leaf gap' left where the leaf's vascular bundle leaves that of the main branch resembles two axes splitting. In each of the four groups to evolve megaphylls, their leaves first evolved during the late Devonian to early Carboniferous, diversifying rapidly until the designs settled down in the mid Carboniferous.

The cessation of further diversification can be attributed to developmental constraints, but why did it take so long for leaves to evolve in the first place? Plants had been on the land for at least 50 million years before megaphylls became significant. However, small, rare mesophylls are known from the early Devonian genus *Eophyllophyton* – so development could not have been a barrier to their appearance. The best explanation so far incorporates observations that atmospheric CO_2 was declining rapidly during this time – falling by around 90 per cent during the Devonian. This corresponded with an increase in stomatal density by 100 times. Stomata allow water to evaporate from leaves, which causes them to curve. It appears that the low stomatal density in the early Devonian meant that evaporation was limited, and leaves would overheat if they grew to any size. The stomatal density could not increase, as the primitive steles and limited root systems would not be able to supply water quickly enough to match the rate of transpiration.

Secondary evolution can also disguise the true evolutionary origin of some leaves. Some genera of ferns display complex leaves which are attached to the pseudostele by an outgrowth of the vascular bundle, leaving no leaf gap. Further, horsetail (*Equisetum*) leaves bear only a single vein, and appear for all the world to be microphyllous; however, in the light of the fossil record and molecular evidence, we conclude that their forbears bore leaves with complex venation, and the current state is a result of secondary simplification.

Deciduous trees deal with another disadvantage to having leaves. The popular belief that plants shed their leaves when the days get too short is misguided; evergreens prospered in the Arctic circle during the most recent greenhouse earth. The generally accepted reason for shedding leaves during winter is to cope with the weather –

the force of wind and weight of snow are much more comfortably weathered without leaves to increase surface area. Seasonal leaf loss has evolved independently several times and is exhibited in the ginkgoales, pinophyta and angiosperms. Leaf loss may also have arisen as a response to pressure from insects; it may have been less costly to lose leaves entirely during the winter or dry season than to continue investing resources in their repair.

Factors Influencing Leaf Architectures

Various physical and physiological forces like light intensity, humidity, temperature, wind speeds etc. are thought to have influenced evolution of leaf shape and size. It is observed that high trees rarely have large leaves, owing to the obstruction they generate for winds. This obstruction can eventually lead to the tearing of leaves, if they are large. Similarly, trees that grow in temperate or taiga regions have pointed leaves, presumably to prevent nucleation of ice onto the leaf surface and reduce water loss due to transpiration. Herbivory, not only by large mammals, but also small insects has been implicated as a driving force in leaf evolution, an example being plants of the genus *Aciphylla*, that are commonly found in New Zealand. The now extinct Moas fed upon these plants, and its seen that the leaves have spines on their bodies, which probably functioned to discourage the moas from feeding on them. Other members of *Aciphylla* that did not co-exist with the moas, do not have these spines.

Genetic Evidences for Leaf Evolution

At the genetic level, developmental studies have shown that repression of the KNOX genes is required for initiation of the leaf primordium. This is brought about by *ARP* genes, which encode transcription factors. Genes of this type have been found in many plants studied till now, and the mechanism i.e. repression of KNOX genes in leaf primordia, seems to be quite conserved. Interestingly, expression of KNOX genes in leaves produces complex leaves. It is speculated that the *ARP* function arose quite early in vascular plant evolution, because members of the primitive group

Lycophytes also have a functionally similar gene Other players that have a conserved role in defining leaf primordia are the phytohormone auxin, gibberelin and cytokinin.

One interesting feature of a plant is its phyllotaxy. The arrangement of leaves on the plant body is such that the plant can maximally harvest light under the given constraints, and hence, one might expect the trait to be genetically robust. However, it may not be so. In maize, a mutation in only one gene called *abphyl (*Abnormal Phyllotaxy) was enough to change the phyllotaxy of the leaves. It implies that sometimes, mutational tweaking of a single locus on the genome is enough to generate diversity. The *abphyl* gene was later on shown to encode a cytokinin response regulator protein.

Once the leaf primordial cells are established from the SAM cells, the new axes for leaf growth are defined, one important (and more studied) among them being the abaxial-adaxial (lower-upper surface) axes. The genes involved in defining this, and the other axes seem to be more or less conserved among higher plants. Proteins of the *HD-ZIPIII* family have been implicated in defining the adaxial identity. These proteins deviate some cells in the leaf primordium from the default abaxial state, and make them adaxial. It is believed that in early plants with leaves, the leaves just had one type of surface - the abaxial one. This is the underside of today's leaves. The definition of the adaxial identity occurred some 200 million years after the abaxial identity was established. One can thus imagine the early leaves as an intermediate stage in evolution of today's leaves, having just arisen from spiny stem-like outgrowths of their leafless ancestors, covered with stomata all over, and not optimized as much for light harvesting. How the infinite variety of plant leaves is generated is a subject of intense research. Some common themes have emerged. One of the most significant is the involvement of KNOX genes in generating compound leaves, as in tomato. But this again is not universal. For example, pea uses a different mechanism for doing the same thing. Mutations in genes affecting leaf curvature can also change leaf form, by changing the leaf from flat, to a crinky shape, like the shape of cabbage leaves. There also exist different morphogen gradients in a developing leaf which define the leaf's axis. Changes in these morphogen gradients may also affect the leaf form. Another very important class of regulators of leaf development are the microRNAs, whose role in this process has just begun to be documented. The coming years should see a rapid development in comparative studies on leaf development, with many EST sequences involved in the process coming online.

The early Devonian landscape was devoid of vegetation taller than waist height. Without the evolution of a robust vascular system, taller heights could not be attained. There was, however, a constant evolutionary pressure to attain greater height. The most obvious advantage is the harvesting of more sunlight for photosynthesis – by overshadowing competitors – but a further advantage is present in spore distribution, as spores (and, later, seeds) can be blown greater distances if they start higher. This may be demonstrated by *Prototaxites*, thought to be a late Silurian fungus reaching eight metres in height.

To attain arborescence, early plants had to develop woody tissue that provided support and water transport. To understand wood, we must know a little of vascular behaviour. The stele of plants undergoing 'secondary growth' is surrounded by the vascular cambium, a ring of cells which produces more xylem (on the inside) and phloem (on the outside). Since xylem cells comprise dead, lignified tissue, subsequent rings of xylem are added to those already present, forming wood.

The first plants to develop this secondary growth, and a woody habit, were apparently the ferns, and as early as the middle Devonian one species, *Wattieza*, had already reached heights of 8 m and a tree-like habit.

Other clades did not take long to develop a tree-like stature; the late Devonian *Archaeopteris*, a precursor to gymnosperms which evolved from the trimerophytes, reached 30 m in height. These progymnosperms were the first plants to develop true wood, grown from a bifacial cambium, of which the first appearance is in the mid Devonian *Rellimia*. True wood is only thought to have evolved once, giving rise to the concept of a 'lignophyte' clade.

These *Archaeopteris* forests were soon supplemented by lycopods, in the form of lepidodendrales, which topped 50m in height and 2m across at the base. These lycopods rose to dominate late Devonian and Carboniferous coal deposits. Lepidodendrales differ from modern trees in exhibiting determinate growth: after building up a reserve of nutrients at a low height, the plants would 'bolt' to a genetically determined height, branch at that level, spread their spores and die. They consisted of 'cheap' wood to allow their rapid growth, with at least half of their stems comprising a pith-filled cavity. Their wood was also generated by a unifacial vascular cambium – it did not produce new phloem, meaning that the trunks could not grow wider over time.

The horsetail *Calamites* was next on the scene, appearing in the Carboniferous. Unlike the modern horsetail *Equisetum*, *Calamites* had a unifacial vascular cambium, allowing them to develop wood and grow to heights in excess of 10 m. They also branched multiple times.

While the form of early trees was similar to that of today's, the groups containing all modern trees had yet to evolve.

The dominant groups today are the gymnosperms, which include the coniferous trees, and the angiosperms, which contain all fruiting and flowering trees. It was long thought that the angiosperms arose from within the gymnosperms, but recent molecular evidence suggests that their living representatives form two distinct groups. The molecular data has yet to be fully reconciled with morphological data, but it is becoming accepted that the morphological support for paraphyly is not especially strong. This would lead to the conclusion that both groups arose from within the pteridosperms, probably as early as the Permian.

The angiosperms and their ancestors played a very small role until they diversified during the Cretaceous. They started out as small, damp-loving organisms in the understory, and have been diversifying ever since the mid Cretaceous, to become the dominant member of non-boreal forests today.

Roots

The roots of lepidodendrales are thought to be functionally equivalent to the stems, as the similar appearance of 'leaf scars' and 'root scars' on these specimens from different species demonstrates.

Roots are important to plants for two main reasons: Firstly, they provide anchorage to the substrate; more importantly, they provide a source of water and nutrients from the soil. Roots allowed plants to grow taller and faster.

The onset of roots also had effects on a global scale. By disturbing the soil, and promoting its acidification (by taking up nutrients such as nitrate and phosphate, they enabled it to weather more deeply, promoting the draw-down of CO_2 with huge implications for climate. These effects may have been so profound they led to a mass extinction.

But how and when did roots evolve in the first place? While there are traces of root-like impressions in fossil soils in the late Silurian, body fossils show the earliest plants to be devoid of roots. Many had tendrils which sprawled along or beneath the ground, with upright axes or thalli dotted here and there, and some even had non-photosynthetic subterranean branches which lacked stomata. The distinction between root and specialised branch is developmental; true roots follow a different developmental trajectory to stems. Further, roots differ in their branching pattern, and in possession of a root cap. So while Silu-Devonian plants such as *Rhynia* and *Horneophyton* possessed the physiological equivalent of roots, roots – defined as organs differentiated from stems – did not arrive until later. Unfortunately, roots are rarely preserved in the fossil record, and our understanding of their evolutionary origin is sparse.

Rhizoids – small structures performing the same role as roots, usually a cell in diametre – probably evolved very early, perhaps even before plants colonised the land; they are recognised in the Characeae, an algal sister group to land plants. That said, rhizoids probably evolved more than once; the rhizines of lichens, for example, perform a similar role. Even some animals (*Lamellibrachia*) have root-like structures!

More advanced structures are common in the Rhynie chert, and many other fossils of comparable early Devonian age bear structures that look like, and acted like, roots. The rhyniophytes bore fine rhizoids, and the trimerophytes and herbaceous lycopods of the chert bore root-like structure penetrating a few centimetres into the soil. However, none of these fossils display all the features borne by modern roots. Roots and root-like structures became increasingly more common and deeper penetrating during the Devonian period, with lycopod trees forming roots around 20 cm long during the Eifelian and Givetian. These were joined by progymnosperms, which rooted up to about a metre deep, during the ensuing Frasnian stage. True gymnosperms and zygopterid ferns also formed shallow rooting systems during the Famennian period.

The rhizomorphs of the lycopods provide a slightly different approach to rooting. They were equivalent to stems, with organs equivalent to leaves performing the role of rootlets. A similar construction is observed in the extant lycopod *Isoetes*, and this appears to be evidence that roots evolved independently at least twice, in the lycophytes and other plants.

A vascular system is indispensable to a rooted plants, as non-photosynthesising roots need a supply of sugars, and a vascular system is required to transport water and nutrients from the roots to the rest of the plant. These plants are little more advanced than their Silurian forbears, without a dedicated root system; however, the flat-lying axes can be clearly seen to have growths similar to the rhizoids of bryophytes today.

By the mid-to-late Devonian, most groups of plants had independently developed a rooting system of some nature. As roots became larger, they could support larger trees, and the soil was weathered to a greater depth. This deeper weathering had effects not only on the aforementioned drawdown of CO_2, but also opened up new habitats for colonisation by fungi and animals.

Roots today have developed to the physical limits. They penetrate many metres of soil to tap the water table. The narrowest roots are a mere 40 µm in diametre, and could not physically transport water if they were any narrower The earliest fossil roots recovered, by contrast, narrowed from 3 mm to under 700 µm in diametre; of course, taphonomy is the ultimate control of what thickness we can see.

The efficiency of many plants' roots is increased via a symbiotic relationship with a fungal partner. The most common are arbuscular mycorrhizae (AM), literally 'tree-like fungal roots'. These comprise fungi which invade some root cells, filling the cell membrane with their hyphae. They feed on the plant's sugars, but return nutrients generated or extracted from the soil (especially phosphate), which the plant would otherwise have no access to.

This symbiosis appears to have evolved early in plant history. AM are found in all plant groups, and 80 per cent of extant vascular plants, suggesting an early ancestry; a "plant"-fungus symbiosis may even have been the step that enabled them to colonise the land,. Such fungi increase the productivity even of simple plants such as liverworts. Indeed, AM are abundant in the Rhynie chert; the association occurred even before there were true roots to colonise, and some have suggested that roots evolved to provide a more comfortable habitat for mycorrhizal fungi.

Early land plants reproduced in the fashion of ferns: spores germinated into small gametophytes, which produced sperm. These would swim across moist soils to find the female organs (archegonia) on the same or another gametophyte, where they would fuse with an ovule to produce an embryo, which would germinate into a sporophyte.

This mode of reproduction restricted early plants to damp environments, moist enough that the sperm could swim to their destination. Therefore, early land plants were constrained to the lowlands, near shores and streams. The development of heterospory freed them from this constraint.

Heterosporic organisms, as their name suggests, bear spores of two sizes – microspores and megaspores. These would germinate to form microgametophytes and megagametophytes, respectively. This system paved the way for seeds: taken to the extreme, the megasporangia could bear only a single megaspore tetrad, and to complete the transition to true seeds, three of the megaspores in the original tetrad could be aborted, leaving one megaspore per megasporangium.

The transition to seeds continued with this megaspore being 'boxed in' to its sporangium while it germinates. Then, the megagametophyte is contained within a waterproof integument, which forms the bulk of the seed. The microgametophyte – a pollen grain which has germinated from a microspore – is employed for dispersal, only releasing its desiccation-prone sperm when it reaches a receptive megagametophyte.

Lycopods

Lycopods go a fair way down the path to seeds without ever crossing the threshold. Fossil lycopod megaspores reaching 1 cm in diametre, and surrounded by vegetative tissue, are known – these even germinate into a megagametophyte *in situ*. However, they fall short of being seeds, since the nucellus, an inner spore-covering layer, does not completely enclose the spore. A very small slit remains, meaning that the seed is still exposed to the atmosphere. This has two consequences – firstly, it means it is not fully resistant to desiccation, and secondly, sperm do not have to 'burrow' to access the archegonia of the megaspore.

Spermatophytes

The first 'spermatophytes' (literally: seed plants) – that is, the first plants to bear true seeds – are called pteridosperms: literally, 'seed ferns', so called because their foliage consisted of fern-like fronds, although they were not closely related to ferns. The oldest fossil evidence of seed plants is of Late Devonian age and they appear to have evolved out of an earlier group known as the progymnosperms. These early seed plants ranged from trees to small, rambling shrubs; like most early progymnosperms, they were woody plants with fern-like foliage. They all bore ovules, but no cones, fruit or similar. While it is difficult to track the early evolution of seeds, we can trace the lineage of the seed ferns from the simple trimerophytes through homosporous Aneurophytes.

This seed model is shared by basically all gymnosperms (literally: 'naked seeds'), most of which encase their seeds in a woody or fleshy (the yew, for example) cone, but none of which fully enclose their seeds. The angiosperms ('vessel seeds') are the only group to fully enclose the seed, in a carpel.

Fully enclosed seeds opened up a new pathway for plants to follow: that of seed dormancy. The embryo, completely isolated from the external atmosphere and hence protected from desiccation, could survive some years of drought before germinating. Gymnosperm seeds from the late Carboniferous have been found to contain embryos, suggesting a lengthy gap between fertilisation and germination. This period is associated with the entry into a greenhouse earth period, with an associated increase in aridity. This suggests that dormancy arose as a response to drier climatic conditions, where it became advantageous to wait for a moist period before germinating. This evolutionary breakthrough appears to have opened a floodgate: previously inhospitable areas, such as dry mountain slopes, could now be tolerated, and were soon covered by trees.

Seeds offered further advantages to their bearers: they increased the success rate of fertilised gametophytes, and because a nutrient store could be 'packaged' in with the embryo, the seeds could germinate rapidly in inhospitable environments, reaching a size where it could fend for itself more quickly. For example, without an endosperm, seedlings growing in arid environments would not have the reserves to grow roots deep enough to reach the water table before they expired from dehydration. Likewise, seeds germinating in a gloomy understory require an additional reserve of energy to quickly grow high enough to capture sufficient light for self-sustenance. A combination of these advantages gave seed plants the ecological edge over the previously dominant genus *Archaeopteris*, thus increasing the biodiversity of early forests.

Flowers are Modified Leaves

Flowers are modified leaves possessed only by the angiosperms, which are relatively late to appear in the fossil record. Flower-like structures first appear in the fossil records some ~130 mya, in the Cretaceous era. Colourful and/or pungent structures surround the cones of plants such as cycads and gnetales, making a strict definition of the term 'flower' elusive.

The main function of a flower is reproduction, which, before the evolution of the flower and angiosperms, was the job of microsporophylls and megasporophylls. A flower can be considered a powerful evolutionary innovation, because its presence allowed the plant world to access new means and mechanisms for reproduction.

The flowering plants have long been assumed to have evolved from within the *gymnosperms*; according to the traditional morphological view, they are closely allied to the gnetales. However, as noted above, recent molecular evidence is at odds to this hypothesis, nd further suggests that gnetales are more closely related to some gymnosperm groups than angiosperms, and that extant gymnosperms form a distinct clade to the angiosperms, the two clades diverging some 300 million years ago.

The relationship of stem groups to the angiosperms is important in determining the evolution of flowers. stem groups provide an insight into the state of earlier 'forks' on the path to the current state. Convergence increases the risk of misidentifying stem groups. Since the protection of the megagametophyte is evolutionarily desirable, probably many separate groups evolved protective encasements independently. In flowers, this protection takes the form of a carpel, evolved from a leaf and recruited into a protective role, shielding the ovules. These ovules are further protected by a double-walled integument.

Penetration of these protective layers needs something more than a free-floating microgametophyte. Angiosperms have pollen grains comprising just three cells. One cell is responsible for drilling down through the integuments, and creating a conduit for the two sperm cells to flow down. The megagametophyte has just seven cells; of these, one fuses with a sperm cell, forming the nucleus of the egg itself, and another joins with the other sperm, and dedicates itself to forming a nutrient-rich endosperm. The other cells take auxiliary roles. This process of 'double fertilisation' is unique and common to all angiosperms.

In the fossil record, there are three intriguing groups which bore flower-like structures. The first is the Permian pteridosperm *Glossopteris*, which already bore recurved leaves resembling carpels. The Triassic *Caytonia* is more flower-like still, with enclosed ovules – but only a single integument. Further, details of their pollen and stamens set them apart from true flowering plants.

The Bennettitales bore remarkably flower-like organs, protected by whorls of bracts which may have played a similar role to the petals and sepals of true flowers; however, these flower-like structures evolved independently, as the Bennettitales are more closely related to cycads and ginkgos than to the angiosperms.

However, no true flowers are found in any groups save those extant today. Most morphological and molecular analyses place *Amborella*, the nymphaeales and Austrobaileyaceae in a basal clade dubbed 'ANA'. This clade appear to have diverged in the early Cretaceous, around 130 million years ago – around the same time as the earliest fossil angiosperm, and just after the first angiosperm-like pollen, 136 million years ago. The magnoliids diverged soon after, and a rapid radiation had produced eudicots and monocots by 125 million years ago. By the end of the Cretaceous 65.5 million years ago, over 50 per cent of today's angiosperm orders had evolved, and the clade accounted for 70 per cent of global species. It was around this time that flowering trees became dominant over conifers.

The features of the basal 'ANA' groups suggest that angiosperms originated in dark, damp, frequently disturbed areas. It appears that the angiosperms remained constrained to such habitats throughout the Cretaceous – occupying the niche of small herbs early in the successional series. This may have restricted their initial significance, but given them the flexibility that accounted for the rapidity of their later diversifications in other habitats.

The family Amborellaceae is regarded as the sister family of all living flowering plants. That means members of this family were most likely the first flowering plants.

It seems that on the level of the organ, the leaf may be the ancestor of the flower, or at least some floral organs. When we mutate some crucial genes involved in flower development, we end up with a cluster of leaf-like structures. Thus, sometime in history, the developmental programme leading to formation of a leaf must have been altered to generate a flower. There probably also exists an overall robust framework within which the floral diversity has been generated. An example of that is a gene called *Leafy (LFY)*, which is involved in flower development in *Arabidopsis thaliana*. The homologs of this gene are found in angiosperms as diverse as tomato, snapdragon, pea, maize and even gymnosperms. Expression of *Arabidopsis thaliana* LFY in distant plants like poplar and citrus also results in flower-production in these plants. The *LFY* gene regulates the expression of some gene belonging to the MADS-box family. These genes, in turn, act as direct controllers of flower development.

Evolution of the MADS-box Family

The members of the MADS-box family of transcription factors play a very important and evolutionarily conserved role in flower development. According to the ABC Model of flower development, three zones - A, B and C - are generated within the developing flower primordium, by the action of some transcription factors, that are members of the MADS-box family. Among these, the functions of the B and C domain genes have been evolutionarily more conserved than the A domain gene. Many of these genes have arisen through gene duplications of ancestral members of this family. Quite a few of them show redundant functions.

The evolution of the MADS-box family has been extensively studied. These genes are present even in pteridophytes, but the spread and diversity is many times higher in angiosperms. There appears to be quite a bit of pattern into how this family has evolved. Consider the evolution of the C-region gene *AGAMOUS (AG)*. It is expressed in today's flowers in the stamens, and the carpel, which are reproductive organs. It's ancestor in gymnosperms also has the same expression pattern. Here, it is expressed in the strobili, an organ that produces pollens or ovules. Similarly, the B-genes' *(AP3 and PI)* ancestors are expressed only in the male organs in gymnosperms. Their descendants in the modern angiosperms also are expressed only in the stamens, the male reproductive organ. Thus, the same, then-existing components were used by the plants in a novel manner to generate the first flower. This is a recurring pattern in evolution.

Factors Influencing Floral Diversity

There is enormous variation in the developmental programmes of plants. For example, grasses possess unique floral structures. The carpels and stamens are surrounded by scale-like lodicules and two bracts the lemma and the palea. Genetic evidence and morphology suggest that lodicules are homologous to eudicot petals. The palea and lemma may be homologous to sepals in other groups, or may be unique grass structures. The genetic evidence is not clear.

Variation in floral structure is typically due to slight changes in the MADS-box genes and their expression pattern.

Another example is that of *Linaria vulgaris*, which has two kinds of flower symmetries-radial and bilateral. These symmetries are due to epigenetic changes in just one gene called *Cycloidea*.

Arabidopsis thaliana has a gene called *Agamous* that plays an important role in defining how many petals and sepals and other organs are generated. Mutations in this gene give rise to the floral meristem obtaining an indeterminate fate, and many floral organs keep on getting produced. We have flowers like roses, carnations and morning glory, for example, that have very dense floral organs. These flowers have been selected by horticulturists since long for increased number of petals. Researchers have found that the morphology of these flowers is because of strong mutations in the *Agamous* homolog in these plants, which leads to them making a large number of petals and sepals. Several studies on diverse plants like petunia, tomato, Impatiens, maize etc. have suggested that the enormous diversity of flowers is a result of small changes in genes controlling their development.

Some of these changes also cause changes in expression patterns of the developmental genes, resulting in different phenotypes. The Floral Genome Project looked at the EST data from various tissues of many flowering plants. The researchers confirmed that the ABC Model of flower development is not conserved across all angiosperms. Sometimes expression domains change, as in the case of many monocots, and also in some basal angiosperms like *Amborella*. Different models of flower development like the *The fading boundaries model*, or the *Overlapping-boundaries model* which propose non-rigid domains of expression, may explain these architectures. There is a possibility that from the basal to the modern angiosperms, the domains of floral architecture have gotten more and more fixed through evolution.

Flowering Time

Another floral feature that has been a subject of natural selection is flowering time. Some plants flower early in their life cycle, others require a period of vernalization before flowering. This decision is based on factors like temperature, light intensity, presence of pollinators and other environmental signals. We know that genes like *Constans (CO), Flowering Locus C* (*FLC*) and *Frigida* regulate integration of environmental signals into the pathway for flower development. Variations in these loci have been associated with flowering time variations between plants. For example, *Arabidopsis thaliana* ecotypes that grow in the cold, temperate regions require prolonged vernalization before they flower, while the tropical varieties, and the most common lab strains, don't. We now know that this variation is due to mutations in the *FLC* and *Frigida* genes, rendering them non-functional.

Quite a few players in this process are conserved across all the plants studied. Sometimes though, despite genetic conservation, the mechanism of action turns out to be different. For example, rice is a short-day plant, while *Arabidopsis thaliana* is a long-day plant. Now, in both plants, the proteins *CO* and *Flowering Locus T (FT)* are present. But in *Arabidopsis thaliana, CO* enhances *FT* production, while in rice, the *CO* homolog represses *FT* production, resulting in completely opposite downstream effects.

Theories of Flower Evolution

There are many theories that propose how flowers evolved. Some of them are described below:

- The *anthophyte theory* was based upon the observation that a gymnospermic group Gnetales has a flower-like ovule. It has partially developed vessels as found in the angiosperms, and the megasporangium is covered by three envelopes, like the ovary structure of angiosperm flowers. However, many other lines of evidence show that Gnetales is not related to angiosperms.

- The *mostly male theory* has a more genetic basis. Proponents of this theory point out that the gymnosperms have two very similar copies of the gene *LFY* while angiosperms just one. Molecular clock analysis has shown that the other *LFY* paralog was lost in angiosperms around the same time as flower fossils become abundant, suggesting that this event might have led to floral evolution. According to this theory, loss of one of the *LFY* paralog led to flowers that were more male, with the ovules being expressed ectopically. These ovules initially performed the function of attracting pollinators, but sometime later, may have been integrated into the core flower.

Photosynthesis is not quite as simple as adding water to CO_2 to produce sugars and oxygen. A complex chemical pathway is involved, facilitated along the way by a range of enzymes and co-enzymes. The enzyme RuBisCO is responsible for 'fixing' CO_2 – that is, it attaches it to a carbon-based molecule to form a sugar, which can be used by the plant, releasing an oxygen molecule along the way. However, the enzyme is notoriously inefficient, and just as effectively will also fix oxygen instead of CO_2 in a process called photorespiration. This is energetically costly as the plant has to use energy to turn the products of photorepsiration back into a form that can react with CO_2.

Concentrating Carbon

C_4 plants evolved carbon concentrating mechanisms. These work by increasing the concentration of CO_2 around RuBisCO, thereby facilitating photosynthesis and decreasing photorespiration. The process of concentrating CO_2 around RuBisCO requires more energy than allowing gases to diffuse, but under certain conditions – i.e. warm temperatures (>25°C), low CO_2 concentrations, or high oxygen concentrations – pays off in terms of the decreased loss of sugars through photorespiration.

One type of C_4 metabolism employs a so-called Kranz anatomy. This transports CO_2 through an outer mesophyll layer, via a range of organic molecules, to the central bundle sheath cells, where the CO_2 is released. In this way, CO_2 is concentrated near the site of RuBisCO operation. Because RuBisCO is operating in an environment with much more CO_2 than it otherwise would be, it performs more efficiently.

A second mechanism, CAM photosynthesis, temporally separates photosynthesis from the action of RuBisCO. RuBisCO only operates during the day, when stomata are sealed and CO_2 is provided by the breakdown of the chemical malate. More CO_2 is then harvested from the atmosphere when stomata open, during the cool, moist nights, reducing water loss.

Evolutionary Record

These two pathways, with the same effect on RuBisCO, evolved a number of times independently – indeed, C_4 alone arose in 18 different plant families. The C_4 construction is most famously used by a subset of grasses, while CAM is employed by many succulents and cacti. The trait appears to have emerged during the Oligocene, around 25 to 32 million years ago; however, they did not become ecologically significant until the Miocene, -1 million years ago. Remarkably, some charcoalified fossils preserve tissue organised into the Kranz anatomy, with intact bundle sheath cells, allowing the presence C_4 metabolism to be identified without doubt at this time. In deducing their distribution and significance, we resort to the use of isotopic markers. C_3 plants preferentially use the lighter of two isotopes of carbon in the atmosphere, ^{12}C, which is more readily involved in the chemical pathways involved in its fixation. Because C_4 metabolism involves a further chemical step, this effect is accentuated. Plant material can be analysed to deduce the ratio of the heavier ^{13}C to ^{12}C. This ratio is denoted $d^{13}C$. C_3 plants are on average around 14 per cent (parts per thousand) lighter than the atmospheric ratio, while C_4 plants are about 28 per cent lighter. The $d^{13}C$ of CAM plants depends on the percentage of carbon fixed at night relative to what is fixed in the day, being closer to C_3 plants if they fix most carbon in the day and closer to C_4 plants if they fix all their carbon at night.

It's troublesome procuring original fossil material in sufficient quantity to analyse the grass itself, but fortunately we have a good proxy: horses. Horses were globally widespread in the period of interest, and browsed almost exclusively on grasses. There's an old phrase in isotope palæontology, 'you are what you eat (plus a little bit)' – this refers to the fact that organisms reflect the isotopic composition of whatever they eat, plus a small adjustment factor. There is a good record of horse teeth throughout the globe, and their $d^{13}C$ has been measured. The record shows a sharp negative inflection around -1 million years ago, during the Messinian, and this is interpreted as the rise of C_4 plants on a global scale.

When is C_4 an advantage?

While C_4 enhances the efficiency of RuBisCO, the concentration of carbon is highly energy intensive. This means that C_4 plants only have an advantage over C_3 organisms in certain conditions: namely, high temperatures and low rainfall. C_4 plants also need high levels of sunlight to thrive. Models suggest that without wildfires removing shade-casting trees and shrubs, there would be no space for C_4 plants. But wildfires have occurred for 400 million years – why did C_4 take so long to arise, and then appear independently so many times? The Carboniferous period (~300 million years ago) had notoriously high oxygen levels – almost enough to allow spontaneous combustion – and very low CO_2, but there is no C_4 isotopic signature to be found. And there doesn't seem to be a sudden trigger for the Miocene rise.

During the Micoene, the atmosphere and climate was relatively stable. If anything, CO_2 increased gradually from 14 to 9 million years ago before settling down to concentrations similar to the Holocene. This suggests that it did not have a key role in invoking C_4 evolution. Grasses themselves (the group which would give rise to the most occurrences of C_4) had probably been around for 60 million years or more, so had had plenty of time to evolve C_4, which in any case is present in a diverse range of groups and thus evolved independently. There is a strong signal of climate change in South Asia; increasing aridity – hence increasing fire frequency and intensity – may have led to an increase in the importance of grasslands. However, this is difficult to reconcile with the North American record. It is possible that the signal is entirely biological, forced by the fire- - driven acceleration of grass evolution – which, both by increasing weathering and incorporating more carbon into sediments, reduced atmospheric CO_2 levels. Finally, there is evidence that the onset of C_4 from 9 to 7 million years ago is a biased signal, which only holds true for North America, from where most samples originate; emerging evidence suggests that grasslands evolved to a dominant state at least 15Ma earlier in South America.

Although we know many secondary metabolites produced by plants, the extent of the same is still unfathomable. Secondary metabolites are essentially low molecular weight compounds, sometimes having complex structures. They function in processes as diverse as immunity, anti-herbivory, pollinator attraction, communication between plants, maintaining symbiotic associations with soil flora, enhancing the rate of fertilization etc., and hence are significant from the evo-devo perspective. The structural and functional diversity of these secondary metabolites across the plant kingdom is vast; it is estimated that hundreds of thousands of enzymes might be involved in this process in the entire of the plant kingdom, with about 15-25 per cent of the genome coding for these enzymes, and every species having its unique arsenal of secondary metabolites. Many of these metabolites are of enormous medical significance to humans.

What is the purpose of having so many secondary metabolites being produced, with a significant chunk of the metabolome devoted to this activity? It is hypothesized that most of these chemicals help in generating immunity, and in consequence, the diversity of these metabolites is a result of a constant war between plants and their parasites. There is evidence that this may be true in many cases. The big question here is the reproductive cost involved in maintaining such an impressive inventory. Various models have been suggested that probe into this aspect of the question, but a consensus on the extent of the cost is lacking. We still cannot predict whether a plant with more secondary metabolites would be better off than other plants in its vicinity.

Secondary metabolite production seems to have arisen quite early during evolution. Even bacteria possess the ability to make these compounds. But they assume more significant roles in life from fungi onwards to plants. In plants they seem to have spread out using different mechanisms like gene duplications, evolution of novel genes etc. Furthermore, studies have shown that diversity in some of these compounds may be positively selected for.

Although the role of novel gene evolution in the evolution of secondary metabolism cannot be denied, there are several examples where new metabolites have been formed by small changes in the reaction. For example, cyanogen glycosides have been proposed to have evolved multiple times in different plant lineages. There are several such instances of convergent evolution. For example, we now know that enzymes for synthesis of limonene – a terpene – are more similar between angiosperms and gymnosperms than to their own terpene synthesis enzymes. This suggests independent evolution of the limonene biosynthetic pathway in these two lineages.

While environmental factors are significantly responsible for evolutionary change, they act merely as agents for natural selection. Change is inherently brought about via phenomena at the genetic level - mutations, chromosomal rearrangements and epigenetic changes. While the general types of mutations hold true across the living world, in plants, some other mechanisms have been implicated as highly significant.

Polyploidy is a very common feature in plants. It is believed that at least half (and probably all) plants are or have been polyploids. Polyploidy leads to genome doubling, thus generating functional redundancy in most genes. The duplicated genes may attain new function, either by changes in expression pattern or changes in activity. Polyploidy and gene duplication are believed to be among the most powerful forces in evolution of plant form. It is not know though, why genome doubling is such a frequent process in plants. One probable reason is the production of large amounts of secondary metabolites in plant cells. Some of them might interfere in the normal process of chromosomal segregation, leading to polypoidy.

In recent times, plants have been shown to possess significant microRNA families, which are conserved across many plant lineages. In comparison to animals, while the number of plant miRNA families are lesser than animals, the size of each family is much larger. The miRNA genes are also much more spread out in the genome than those in animals, where we find them clustered. It has been proposed that these miRNA families have expanded by duplications of chromosomal regions. Many miRNA genes involved in regulation of plant development have been found to be quite conserved between plants studied.

Domestication of plants like maize, rice, barley, wheat etc. has also been a significant driving force in their evolution. Some studies have tried to look at the origins of the maize plant and it turns out that maize is a domesticated derivative of a wild plant from Mexico called teosinte. Teosinte belongs to the genus *Zea*, just as maize, but bears very small inflorescence, 5-10 hard cobs and a highly branched and spread out stem.

Interestingly, crosses between a particular teosinte variety and maize yields fertile offsprings that are intermediate in phenotype between maize and teosinte. QTL analysis has also revealed some loci that when mutated in maize yield a teosinte-like stem or teosinte-like cobs. Molecular clock analysis of these genes estimates their origins to some 9000 years ago, well in accordance with other records of maize domestication. It is believed that a small group of farmers must have selected some maize-like natural mutant of teosinte some 9000 years ago in Mexico, and subjected it to continuous selection to yield the maize plant as we know today.

Another interesting case is that of cauliflower. The edible cauliflower is a domesticated version of the wild plant *Brassica oleracea*, which does not possess the dense undifferentiated inflorescence called the curd, that cauliflower possesses.

Cauliflower possesses a single mutation in a gene called *CAL*, controlling meristem differentiation into inflorescence. This causes the cells at the floral meristem to gain an undifferentiated identity, and instead of growing into a flower, they grow into a lump of undifferentiated cells. This mutation has been selected through domestication at least since the Greek empire.

Bibliography

Dayton, P.K. M.J. Tegner, P.B. Edwards and K.L. Riser. 1999. Temporal and Spatial Scales of Kelp Demography: The Role of the Oceanographic Climate. *Ecological Monographs* 69: 219-250.

Forest, Noun. *The American Heritage Dictionary of the English Language* (3 ed.). Boston: Houghton Mifflin Company. 1996. ISBN 0-395-44895-6.

Graham, M.H. 2004. Effects of Local Deforestation on the Diversity and Structure of Southern California Giant Kelp Forest Food Webs. *Ecosystems* 7: 341-357.

Harrold, C. and D.C. Reed. 1985. Food Availability, Sea Urchin Grazing and Kelp Forest Community Structure. *Ecology* 66: 1160-1169.

Jenkins Martin D., Groombridge Brian, *World Atlas of Biodiversity: Earth's Living Resources in the 21st Century*, World Conservation Monitoring Centre, United Nations Environment Programme, retrieved 20 March 2007.

Joly, A.B. and E.C. Oliveira Filho. 1967. Two Brazilian *Laminarias*. Instituto de Pesquisas da Marinha 4: 1-7.

Jones, C.G., J.H. Lawton and M. Shachak. 1997. Positive and Negative Effects of Organisms as Physical Ecosystem Engineers. *Ecology* 78: 1946-1957

Lund, H. Gyde 2006. 'Definitions of Forest, Deforestation, Afforestation, and Reforestation'. Gainesville, VA: Forest Information Services.

Mann, K.H. 1973. Seaweeds: Their Productivity and Strategy for Growth. *Science* 182: 975-981.

United Nations Environment Programme, *World Conservation Monitoring Centre, Background to Forest Mapping & Data Harmonisation*, retrieved 20 March 2007.

Santelices, B. 2007. The Discovery of Kelp Forests in Deep-water Habitats of Tropical Regions. *Proceedings of the NationalAwan Riak Academy of Sciences* 104: 19163-19164.

What is a Forest?". *Australian Government/Department of Agriculture, Fisheries, and Forestry/Rural Areas.* March 28, 2007.

Wildlife defies Chernobyl Radiation, by Stefen Mulvey, BBC News April 20, 2006.

World Resources Institute, 1997. The Last Frontier Forests: Ecosystems and Economies on the Edge.

Index